Contents

Introduction

Developing rich Internet applications (RIAs), web applications that look and function like traditional desktop applications, can often be a complex and difficult process. Ensuring your application looks right and works as expected is not easy. Initial solutions relied on browser plug-ins and specific scripting languages, but since the release of Google Web Toolkit (GWT) and related RIA widget frameworks such as Ext GWT, RIA development is now easier and more flexible. So, if you can build Java applications, you can quickly build an enterprise-class rich Internet application.

Focusing on everything you need to know about Ext GWT, this book will show you the tasks necessary to build enterprise-class rich Internet applications. I will assume you are familiar with Java and only need a crash course in GWT—after all, I'd rather be showing you how to use some neat and clever widget as part of a rich Internet application. So let's get into it.

This Book's Audience

This book is for enterprise Java developers who have a need to rapidly gain high-quality results in the RIA space using Ext GWT. This book also offers some insight on Ext GWT to the casual developers who are looking to add that "enterprise-RIA" look to their existing GWT application.

This book was written when Ext GWT 2.0 was nearing release and is based on GWT 1.6; this book contains information on the most current and recent available RIA technologies.

Getting the Example Code

All of the example code, including instructions on how to use it, is available in the Source Code page of the Apress web site (http://www.apress.com).

About the Author

Grant Slender has been an IT instructor, engineer, consultant, and developer since 1995. His first exposure to Java was in 1997 when he attended a Sun Microsystems training course, and he has been a loyal follower ever since. After observing Google's success with GWT, he started looking for a widget library that would complement and extend it. In 2007, he discovered Ext GWT and has become an active contributor to the community, producing several custom widgets. He currently provides consulting services specializing in Ext GWT.

Grant can be reached by sending an e-mail to gslender@gmail.com.

Chapter 1: Overview of Ext GWT and GWT

Ext GWT and GWT are a powerful combination that can produce some amazing looking and performing web applications. Java developers looking for an RIA framework where they can leverage their existing investment and knowledge in tools and libraries will really appreciate Ext GWT.

You will be able to use your existing knowledge in development environments, build tools, and web application servlet containers and be right at home with Ext GWT. Throughout this book, I will be introducing and using the popular Eclipse Java IDE, but you should be able to use any similar set of tools that you feel more comfortable with.

This chapter will provide you with an outline of Ext GWT, a quick overview of its features, and a little bit of background information. I will also provide a quick overview of GWT, and a crash course introduction into how it works and how applications are assembled.

About Ext GWT

Ext GWT (also shortened as GXT) is a GWT-based enterprise widget framework built by ExtJS (http://www.extjs.com), the company that developed the highly popular JavaScript library of the same name. As an extension to Google's toolkit, GXT adds a wealth of enterprise-grade interactive widgets, layouts, and template classes, a complete data model and caching store, and a model-view-controller (MVC) application framework.

Starting life as an open source project named "MyGWT," the project's lead developer joined ExtJS and further expanded the library, rewriting many aspects of the original framework. Now at version 2.0, GXT boasts an impressive set of features designed to fast-track RIA development.

Following is a short summary of these features:

- Grids, list and data views, trees, and tables for displaying and editing data.

- Framed and tabbed panels, and layout managers to border and arrange things in.

- Enhanced windows, dialogs, and message/alert and information boxes.

- Forms with plain and rich text editors, number, and password fields; combo drop-down boxes; time and date calendar; and radio and check boxes.

- Buttons, tool tips, toolbars, status bars, and menu bars.

- Local caching stores, loaders, and data models to ensure data can be simply managed via widgets.

- Advanced user interface options for desktop and portal applications, including an MVC framework.

- A range of miscellaneous effects, such as resizable and dragable options for widgets and containers.

EXT GWT FACTS

Pronouncing Ext GWT: While not official, the most common pronunciation is "e-x-t g-w-t," which aligns with how most folks pronounce ExtJS and GWT.

Mixing Ext GWT and ExtJS: Ext GWT was designed to be used only with GWT. Mixing other JavaScript libraries (even ExtJS) may cause unpredictable results, and therefore isn't recommended.

Licensing: Ext GWT is dual licensed and available under an open source GPL v3 license, as well as a commercial license for those who don't wish to, or can't, comply with GPL terms.

Native: Ext GWT is a 100 percent pure GWT solution, and the majority of the browser page manipulation is conducted through GWT's classes and methods. Ext GWT is not just a thin wrapper around the existing ExtJS JavaScript library.

Supported browsers: Ext GWT supports all major web browsers, including Internet Explorer 6+, FireFox 1.5+ (PC, Mac), Safari 3+, and Opera 9+ (PC, Mac).

Like all GWT libraries, development with GXT is performed using the Java programming language. While GXT is suited to web development, you won't need any extensive knowledge of HTML, cascading style sheets (CSS), or JavaScript, which is great for experienced enterprise Java developers. If this is you, then you'll be right at home building professional web applications after only a small amount of time.

Like all GWT applications, GXT is compiled from Java source into JavaScript and combined with HTML and CSS files to produce a self-contained web application. This process ensures that your application code, and the GXT library itself, is tightly coupled and compiled using the best-known JavaScript optimization techniques available for each individual browser. This "compiling to JavaScript" approach can produce faster and more efficient JavaScript than you can by hand—unless you have kung fu JavaScript skills, in which case you're probably already working for Google.

About GWT

Google released the first version of GWT in May 2006. Now at version 1.6, GWT has considerable features that help create interactive web applications. An open source project, released under an Apache 2.0 license, GWT is openly and actively developed by the Google team. It has enjoyed ongoing support and development, with bug fixes and updates released regularly.

Without doubt, GWT is a library designed to facilitate fast and efficient Ajax (asynchronous JavaScript and XML) development. Unfortunately, on its own it falls short as a *complete* rich Internet application toolkit, as it lacks rich widgets and an appropriate application framework.

Following is a short summary of these features:

- Full Java 5 language support (such as generics, enumerated types, annotations, etc.).

- A Java-to-JavaScript compiler with hosted mode emulation, allowing full support for Java debugging.

- Browser independence—quirks and history management issues are dramatically reduced.

- Basic widget support for buttons; forms; elements; simple tables; and tree widgets, dialogs, and panels.

- Support for a range of server integration and communication options (RPC, XML, or JSON).

- JUnit testing support and integration.

- Internationalization language and locale support.

Note   The terms *Ajax* and *RIA* are often used interchangeably to mean an interactive web application, but I have decided to create a distinction whereby browser interactions alone would not equate to a rich Internet application. Thus, Ajax is used to refer to the ability to manipulate the contents of the browser, utilize the XMLHttpRequest object for server asynchronous requests, and react to user input. RIA is used to refer to a more "desktop-like" visual experience that leverages Ajax, combined with complex and enhanced widgets that can also manipulate data and respond to user actions.

A sound knowledge of Java is required to successfully develop GWT applications, although you will only need to use a subset of the Java API. In saying that, on the server side of your application, you may need to construct a typical J2EE web framework, or find some alternative web platform in another language that provides a similar degree of functionality. GWT (and GXT) will happily support any server platform and language.

GWT provides emulated support for java.lang, java.util, and certain classes within java.io and java.sql packages, but not for anything outside of this. As GWT compiles Java source into JavaScript targeted to run in a browser, it wouldn't make sense to support many of the advanced Java API features such as advanced IO, networking, JDBC, and Swing packages. Using many of the other aspects of the Java API (like reflection) is just not possible, as they would need to be emulated in JavaScript.

Given that GWT is focused around producing web applications on a browser, most of what you need to do is provided by the GWT packages.

GWT Crash Course

As GXT development is an extension of GWT, with advanced widgets and a complete application framework, it is probably worthwhile to review how a GWT application works and how it's assembled. If you're already familiar with GWT, you can skip this section and jump straight to Chapter 2.

How Does It Work?

GWT applications start life as Java source code, and whether compiled or emulated by the hosted mode shell, they are converted into an equivalent JavaScript application. These JavaScript applications are monolithic, meaning they execute as a single application, and do not require access to a web server to interact with the user. This is dramatically different from normal web applications that constantly refresh the browser's page, requesting further content as the user interacts with the application.

Thinking back to traditional web applications, a user requests a page and the server responds with a dynamically generated page response. As the user interacts with the web site, there are multiple page requests and subsequent delays as the user has to wait for the server to respond. The web application is constructed using multiple pages, with each functional part of the application served as a dynamic page and sent to the browser.

When using GWT, the entire application can be loaded at once, and all interaction is performed without requiring further requests to and from the server. GWT manipulates the underlying browser Document Object Model (DOM) using JavaScript to dynamically render a page and add and adjust various widgets (buttons, fields, tables, etc.). User interaction events are detected, and this allows the application to update the DOM and respond with the results. If no data needs to be persisted, the entire web application can be served to the user's browser without any further server requests.

Tip   It's worth seeing firsthand how powerful it can be to build a web application that doesn't need to always contact the web server for user interaction. A popular GWT game, GSudokr (http://www.gsudokr.com), is a good example where the entire application is loaded and all interaction occurs without any further server requests.

When data needs to be sent or retrieved from the server, GWT applications communicate with servers asynchronously (meaning without disrupting end-user interactions). This ability to interact with the user without waiting on the server, and still being able to request and save data back again, is a fundamental Ajax feature.

GWT provides this server communication using Remote Procedure Call (RPC). RPC provides a seamless solution that allows Java objects to be passed between server and client. The use of RPC allows both client and server to be developed as a single Java application. RPC removes the need for object transformation, as plain old Java objects (POJOs) can be serialized and transferred to and from the client.

Alternatively, GWT also offers support for XML and JSON data, for when you need to interact with non-Java web servers, or don't wish to use RPC in an existing Java web application.

How Is It Developed?

During normal development, you will often want to run and test various aspects of the application to ensure the code is working as expected. To avoid a continuous recompiling, GWT includes a combined "browser client and web server" shell that interprets the Java code in real time and interacts with the DOM, thus simulating what would occur when compiled.

This emulated browser and server mode is simply called *hosted mode*. You will spend most of your development time in hosted mode. When final JavaScript deployment is required, you compile and run the final web application in a normal browser; this is commonly called *web mode*.

Tip   Hosted mode actually uses a native browser to render, so any browser quirks in hosted mode might show differently when run in web mode on another browser. For example, on Windows platforms, the Internet Explorer browser is plugged into the hosted mode shell. On rare occasions, it is possible that issues may not show up until the application is tested on another browser in web mode. In saying that, GXT does a pretty good job of ensuring all widgets behave the same way across all supported browsers, so coding can be reliably preformed in hosted mode with final testing for all browsers left to web mode.

One significant benefit of working in hosted mode is that you can *code-test-debug* your application all in a Java development environment along with your favorite Java debugger. You can step right through the code, seeing the results and changes appear, right in the browser. This approach provides a rapid development process and limits the need to compile the entire application until you are ready to build a release and perform extensive browser testing.

How Is It Deployed?

GWT requires Java source code and files to be organized and structured a particular way, and I'll cover this in the next chapter. As a way of introduction, GWT expects to find Java source files in a package name that includes .client. in the full package name. An XML document (called a GWT module file) must exist that identifies an entry point for where the application begins, and your public resource files are expected to exist either in the war folder or in the .public. package.

All this is done to ensure the GWT compiler can resolve dependencies, compile, and link your project into a set of JavaScript, CSS, HTML, and resource files (images, etc.). Luckily, GWT includes a few application and project setup scripts to help create this required file structure, and automatically builds source templates to get you started quickly.

The entire compile process parses the source files, generates the required output, and assembles them as a matched set of output files so that they can be hosted and served without further postproduction effort. If you don't communicate with the server, you can now deploy this set of web files onto any web server or just run them locally; it's just static HTML, JavaScript, and resource files.

If you are using GWT RPC, then you'll need to bundle up your server-side classes and deploy to any Java-compatible servlet container. Obviously, on the server side of things, it can get a little more complex, but essentially for GWT, most of the requirements are simple and will be covered in full detail in later chapters.

Note   GWT requires a paradigm shift from traditional web application design. Typically, in most web applications, the developer or web framework must ensure the application state is managed as part of a web server task. Pages are requested and refreshed upon every client application state change, and these round-trip requests need to be managed as part of the web server application state. This web server task is not required for GWT applications; the application state is 100 percent client side and does not require interaction with a web server.

Rethinking is required for those who come from a web application background. Don't design your rich Internet application like a traditional web application.

Summary

With this overview of GXT and GWT behind you, you should now have a good understanding of what to expect out of each library and toolkit. You have also been given a quick refresh and introduction to how GWT works, what to expect when you start developing, and how things will be deployed.

The next chapter will assist you with what you'll need to get started with GXT, ensuring your development environment is ready to begin development and testing, and what you can do to help with final deployment.

Chapter 2: Organizing the Environment

Organizing your development environment for GXT is no different than preparing for GWT development. There are only a few additional steps beyond basic GWT preparation to ensure the GXT library is included in the development and build processes. This chapter will take you through understanding the basic ingredients, show you how to set up and prepare the Eclipse IDE, and leave you with a skeleton project structure that can be used to start any rich Internet application (RIA) development.

The Basic Ingredients

Building RIAs with GXT requires some fresh ingredients that you can simply download and mix together to produce a delicious RIA cake *(mmm, so very tasty)*. GWT takes advantage of Java and its extensive range of tools, and so the list of items in Table 2-1 includes Java and the common development tools used in conjunction with GXT.

Throughout this book I'll be providing code listings that have all been tested against the versions of tools and libraries outlined here. To ensure you don't run into any unforeseen issues, please download and install at least these versions (or later), unless you are confident you can sort out the differences yourself.

Table 2-1. The List of Items You'll Need to Download

DOWNLOAD	DESCRIPTION	WEB SITE
JDK6	The Java SE Development Kit (JDK) includes the Java runtime and command-line development tools.	http://java.sun.com
Eclipse 3.4.1	The Eclipse IDE includes a Java compiler, debugger, syntax highlighting editor, and other various plug-ins and tools.	http://www.eclipse.org
GWT 1.6	The Google Web Toolkit includes a hosted mode shell, Java-to-JavaScript compiler, setup scripts, and the GWT library.	http://code.google.com/web toolkit/
GXT 2.0	The GXT framework includes a source, a compiled library, and examples.	http://www.extjs.com/ products/gxt/

Tip   Eclipse includes bundled Ant and CVS/SVN support and does not require specifically downloading those popular tools. Eclipse is also available in a version for Java EE developers. This Java EE version includes support for J2EE features and common web development tasks, such as cascading style sheets (CSS) and HTML editors. While not mandatory for RIA development, you'll probably appreciate the benefit of having these extra tools.

GWT provides out-of-the-box support for creating Eclipse projects. Technically, you can use any Java development environment, but I've decided to focus on Eclipse as the tool of choice. I'm using the Windows platform for development, but you should be able to use any of the supported GWT platforms.

Setting Up Eclipse

Before I begin creating our first GXT project, I need to configure a few things within Eclipse that will make working with GXT a little easier.

The only preliminary requirement is to install the Java software development kit (SDK) and unzip Eclipse, GWT, and GXT. I'll assume you're able to do this without instructions and that you have verified that Eclipse can run, compile, and debug a normal Java project. If you're unable to get this working, then you should really solve this problem before continuing.

Defining User Libraries

Both GWT and GXT JAR files need to be added to the Java build path within any project. A good way of doing this is to create an Eclipse user library. In Eclipse, choose Window ➤ Preferences. In the Java section, choose Build Path and then User Libraries.

You should now create two new user libraries, the first titled GWT_1_6 for GWT and the second titled GXT_2_0 for GXT. Now add the associated JAR files for each library (two for GWT and just one for GXT). When completed, the user libraries you have defined should be similar to those shown in Figure 2-1.

Figure 2-1. GWT and GXT user libraries defined

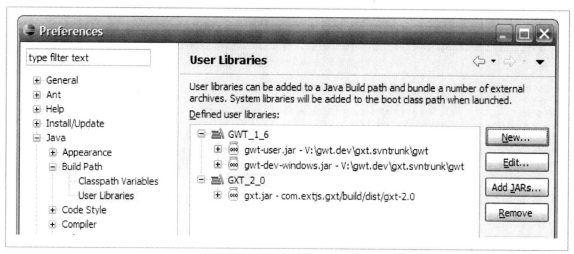

Tip   If you intend to build and run GWT applications outside of Eclipse, you'll probably need a simple way to add those JAR files to any project classpath. The best way is via your platform's system environment variables, so you may wish to create something like GWT_HOME and GXT_HOME. It's also worthwhile to add the GWT_HOME path location to the system path so that you can easily use the command-line tools.

Creating an Application

To begin any project, you'll need to organize and structure a few files, directories, and configuration options. GWT includes some scripts that automatically do this for you and also populate your application with template code that acts as a good starting point for development.

To begin, create an Eclipse project with the GWT command tool webAppCreator. This tool will create the required project files that can be imported into Eclipse. This is a fairly simple tool, and all command options are shown in Table 2-2.

Table 2-2. The webAppCreator Command Options

OPTION	DESCRIPTION
-out	The directory to write output files into (defaults to current)
-overwrite	Overwrite any existing files
-ignore	Ignore any existing files; do not overwrite
moduleName	The name of the module to create (fully qualified Java class name)

As an example, the following command creates GWT files for an Eclipse project called myApp, and puts them in a directory called myApp:

```
webAppCreator -out myApp com.apress.MyApp
```

Importing to Eclipse

Now that your project and application have been created, you can import them into the Eclipse workspace. Choose File ➤ Import, and then select Existing Projects into Workspace. Choose the myApp folder, and click Finish.

You should now have a GWT application project within Eclipse that you can launch and test. To launch the GWT application, open the project, find the MyApp.launch file, and right-click it. Then choose Run As ➤ MyApp, and you should see the GWT hosted mode shell, similar to Figure 2-2.

Figure 2-2. Hosted mode shell running GWT MyApp

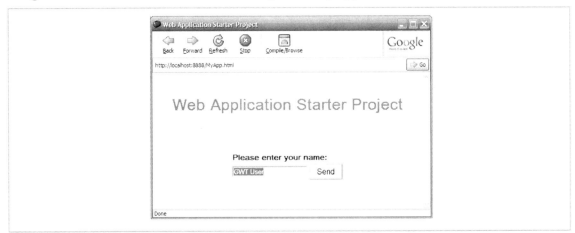

Adjusting for GXT

The preceding sections established a GWT application project, and now the final step is to adjust a few things to accommodate GXT. This primarily involves some minor changes to the gwt.xml module file, cleaning up the HTML file, copying resources, and including a JAR library file.

Including the Libraries

You'll need to ensure the GXT library (GXT_2_0) is included in both the build path of the project and the classpath of the launch configuration.

1. **Build path:** Right-click the MyApp project and choose Properties. Click Java Build Path. Under the Libraries tab, add a Library, choose User Library, and then select the GXT_2_0 library. You can also remove the GWT JAR files and add the GWT_1_6 user library.

2. **Classpath:** Right-click the MyApp.launch file, and choose Run As ➤ Run Configurations. Ensure the MyApp.launch file is selected. Under Classpath, select User Entries, and then click Advanced. Choose Add Library, and then select the GXT_2_0 library. You can also remove the GWT JAR files and add the GWT_1_6 user library, as shown in Figure 2-3.

Figure 2-3. Configuring the classpath for the MyApp.launch file

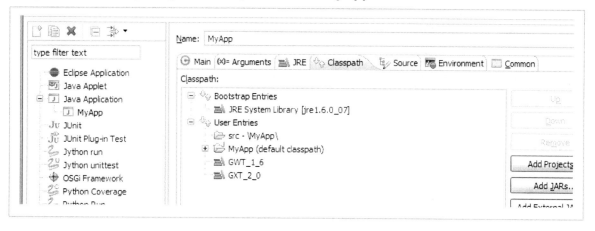

Caution   It is easy to get all these classpath requirements mixed up and confused, so take care when removing and adding things. Remember that GWT requires a path to source files, not just compiled class files—that is why all GWT JAR files contain source code as well as compiled class files.

So, if you add another GWT project to the path, you'll also need to ensure the source folder is included, something that isn't so obvious when you're trying to figure out why the GWT shell won't run.

Changing the GWT Module File

You now need to update the project's module file (MyApp.gwt.xml), located in the com.apress package, and tell GWT to inherit the GXT library file. The webAppCreator adds a few extra items in the module xml file that you won't need for a basic GXT application. After you add the GXT module inheritance and strip out the unnecessary lines, the module file looks as follows:

```
<?xml version="1.0" encoding="UTF-8"?>
<!DOCTYPE module PUBLIC "-//Google Inc.//DTD Google Web Toolkit 1.6.1//EN"
"http://google-web-toolkit.googlecode.com
/svn/tags/1.6.1/distro-source/core/src/gwt-module.dtd">
<module rename-to='myapp'>
  <inherits name='com.extjs.gxt.ui.GXT'/>
  <entry-point class='com.apress.client.MyApp'/>
</module>
```

Note   The GXT module file will inherit all the needed GWT libraries, so you don't have to include them in your project's module xml file. There is nothing wrong with keeping them, but to keep it nice and simple, it is OK to remove them here.

Cleaning Up the HTML Host File

The next task is to ensure the HTML file is organized to support GXT. In GWT 1.6, the HTML file is located in the root of the war folder.

For GXT, you should ensure the correct doctype is defined and that you're including all the needed style sheets.

- Ensure the following doctype is defined:

```
<!DOCTYPE HTML PUBLIC "-//W3C//DTD HTML 4.01 Transitional//EN">
```

- Add the following style sheets to your host page:

```
<link rel="stylesheet" type="text/css" href="css/ext-all.css" />
```

Note　　　　To ensure the widgets are rendered correctly, GXT requires the browser to be in quirks mode (as opposed to the stricter standard mode). See http://en.wikipedia.org/wiki/Quirks_mode for more information on the various browser-rendering modes.

Once again you can trim out all the unnecessary lines within the HTML host file. When completed, your HTML file will look similar to Listing 2-1.

Listing 2-1. MyApp.html

```
<!DOCTYPE HTML PUBLIC "-//W3C//DTD HTML 4.01 Transitional//EN">
<html>
  <head>
    <link type="text/css" rel="stylesheet" href="MyApp.css">
    <link type="text/css" rel="stylesheet" href="css/gxt-all.css" />
    <title>MyApp</title>
    <script type="text/javascript" language="javascript"
src="myapp/myapp.nocache.js"></script>
  </head>
  <body>
  </body>
</html>
```

Copying Resources

The final task is to copy the resources from the GXT download into your war folder. As we used the path of gxt with the style sheet paths, you'll need to copy these CSS files and image resources into the war/gxt folder.

Tip When developing large GWT applications, you may need to ensure the Java VM has enough memory to compile. To ensure this, set the VM arguments in the launch configuration to -Xmx512M -Xss64m. This will give 512MB of memory to the heap and 64MB to the stack, which should be enough for most medium RIAs. Obviously, larger applications may need more to compile.

My First GXT App

The template Java source code created by the webAppCreator GWT tool obviously doesn't create any GXT widgets. To test that everything is working, you'll need to add some code that is purely GXT.

Listing 2-2 places a button onto the page. When you click the button, an alert message box shows.

Listing 2-2. MyApp.java

```
package com.apress.client;

import com.extjs.gxt.ui.client.event.*;
import com.extjs.gxt.ui.client.widget.MessageBox;
import com.extjs.gxt.ui.client.widget.button.Button;
import com.google.gwt.core.client.EntryPoint;
import com.google.gwt.user.client.ui.RootPanel;

public class MyApp implements EntryPoint {
  public void onModuleLoad() {
    Button b = new Button("Click me...");
    SelectionListener< ButtonEvent> sl;
    sl = new SelectionListener<ButtonEvent>() {
      public void componentSelected(ButtonEventce) {
        MessageBox.alert("Button Pressed",
            "You pressed the button", null);
      }
    };
    b.addSelectionListener(sl);
    RootPanel.get().add(b);
  }
}
```

After applying these changes to the source code, you should be able to run the application and get a result similar to Figure 2-4.

Figure 2-4. Hosted mode shell running GXT MyApp

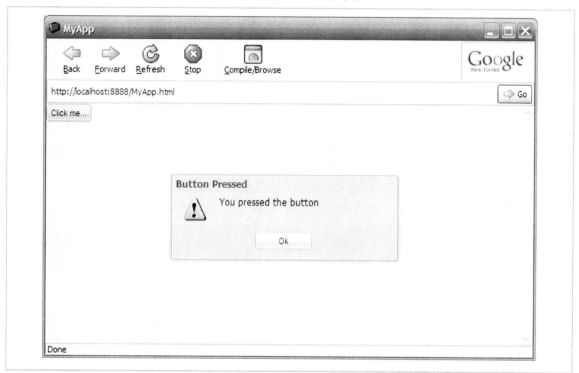

Summary

Like all building projects, taking the time to set up your tools and prepare your working environment often pays dividends in the end. After reading this chapter, you know the tools needed and the steps required to organize the development environment for GXT. As a nice bonus, you have built and launched your first GXT application. Awesome—only the second chapter, and you've built a rich Internet application. Told you it was easy!

Chapter 3 covers the large number of widgets, how to use them, and some tips and tricks. You'll also get a chance to add theme support to give your applications that unique and styled look.

Chapter 3: Widgets, Widgets, Everywhere

Like any library intended to help build rich Internet applications (RIAs), having an extensive range of widgets is highly desirable. True to its cause, GXT packs plenty of RIA goodness—more than 10 separate packages with over 210 classes dedicated to widgets. Each widget is rich with configurable options and comes theme-ready, allowing you to pick from the many available themes or design your own look to match your needs. Figure 3-1 illustrates the online Explorer demo, which showcases many of the available widgets and is a good way to understand what is possible with GXT.

Figure 3-1. Explorer showcasing some of the GXT widgets

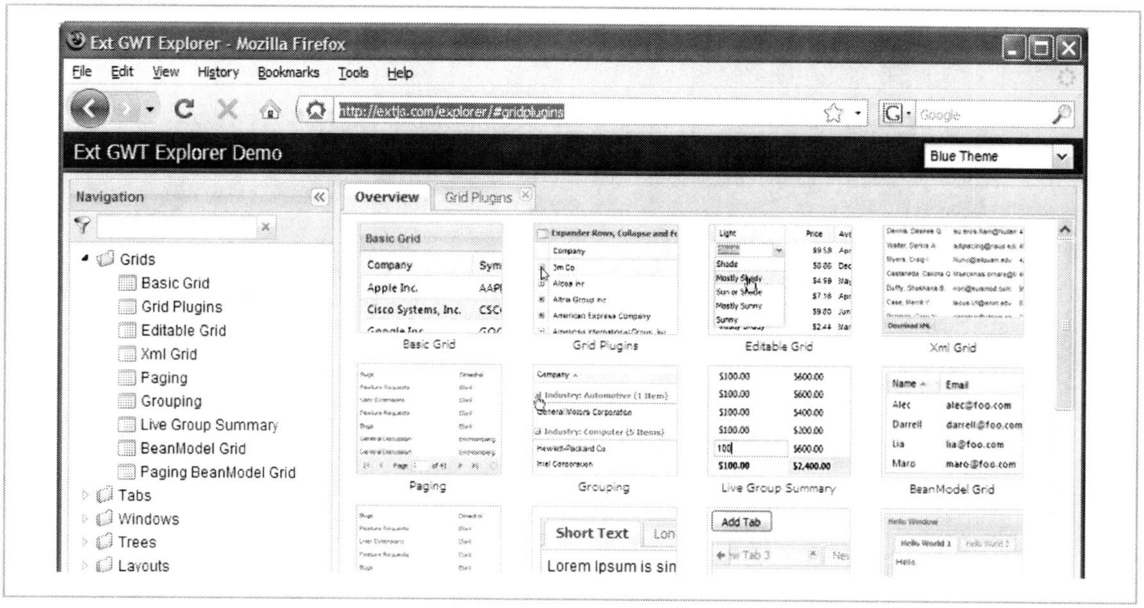

This is the chapter where you will be spending most of your time, learning about the widgets, how to use them, and what is possible. I'll start with an overview of all the widgets and then cover code listings for most of the common widgets. I'll also outline any tricks or important gotchas you'll face when developing an application.

The Complete Ext-ended Family

All widgets are found in the com.extjs.gxt.ui.client.widget package and are structurally grouped as outlined in Figure 3-2.

Figure 3-2. GXT's extensive library of widgets

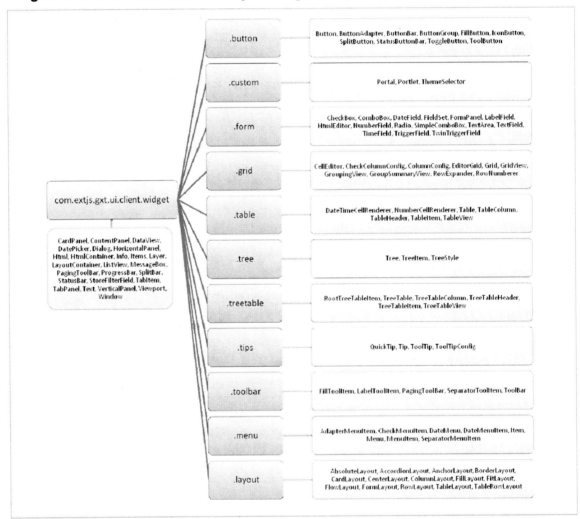

THE SOURCE CODE

This book comes with all the code used in the listings and examples ready to run. The GWT module called CodeSnippet contains all the utility methods used throughout the book and a list of all the code listing methods for each chapter. Each chapter's code listings are bundled together into a chapter class, such as Chapter3. If you set up the GWT_1_6 and GXT_2_0 user libraries correctly within Eclipse, you should be able to just launch the CodeSnippet file.

All of the code listing methods are commented so that they can't all run at once. You only need to uncomment one of the methods to see the listing in action. *Remember to uncomment only one method at a time, or strange things could happen!*

Chapter 6 pulls the things shown in this book into a complete and functional application. The application builds on top of the MyApp module, with some changes made to various configuration files to ensure the application looks and behaves as expected. These changes are also explained.

.widget

The base package, com.extjs.gxt.ui.client.widget, is where most of the base component classes, containers, and general-purpose widgets are found. You would typically start your application with one of the many widgets found in this package.

Component

All GXT widgets use Component as their base class and either extend Component directly or extend BoxComponent if they need support for sizing or positioning. All subclasses of Component can automatically participate in the standard GXT Component life cycle of creation (attach and detach). They also have automatic support for basic hide/show and enable/disable behavior. Component allows any subclass to use lazy rendering into any GXT Container. GXT Containers render children when the layout executes. In some cases, this will only render the visible widgets that are active.

Component itself extends the GWT Widget object, and this allows you to insert and use GXT widgets in GWT applications. Components added to a GWT Panel will be rendered when inserted.

Component handles all the life-cycle aspects of widget creation, attaching and detaching from the Document Object Model (DOM). Component also provides all the basic support for things like lazy rendering, tool tips, hide/show, and enable/disable.

An important aspect of Component (and every widget) is the wrapped El instance you can obtain via the el() method. An El represents an element in the DOM. Using El, you can change style information and adjust size, position, and many other attributes of the element representing the widget. El is similar to GWT's Element and provides a bunch of utility methods for DOM manipulation; think of it like Element on steroids.

How Things Are Rendered

Rendering a widget in GXT is slightly different than in GWT.

In GWT, when a widget is created, usually while calling setElement(Element), it is inserted into the DOM. This occurs when an element is added to a GWT Panel.

A GXT widget is constructed (or rendered) when the onRender method is called. In a GXT Container, this occurs at layout. In a GWT Panel, this occurs immediately (like with GWT widgets).

DEALING WITH RENDERING ISSUES

When you're developing rich Internet applications, you may occasionally be faced with rendering issues where it is hard to uncover the root cause of the problem. Sometimes it's the way you applied the widgets or the order of styles, or you may have simply discovered a bug that nobody else has yet to see—all of which can be hard to work out without knowing exactly what the browser is being asked to do. As such, you are going to need a debug tool that can tell you what exact style or HTML code is being applied to the DOM.

While working in web mode, you can use the Firebug add-on within Firefox or the IE Developer Toolbar add-on for Internet Explorer. Using these tools, you can see what style is being applied and what HTML is being rendered. Unfortunately, there is no hosted-mode tool available, so you need to compile to web mode within GWT to use these browser-based debug tools.

I strongly recommend you always have Firebug or the IE Developer Toolbar handy and ready to test any rendering problems associated with GXT. Firebug can be downloaded from http://getfirebug.com/.

Another important aspect in the rendering process is that some widgets have pre-render attributes. Pre-render attributes set some visual aspect or feature that needs to be defined before the widget is rendered. Methods that require setting pre-render attributes are identified as having the pre-render keyword in their Javadocs.

Events

Events are used throughout GXT to provide the programmer with notifications of the changing state of widgets and user interactions, and as responses to server communications. The event model used should be fairly familiar to any seasoned Java programmer. The typical Observer pattern is used, whereby you add listeners to particular events, and when the event is triggered, the listeners are notified to handle the event.

An entire package, com.extjs.gxt.ui.client.event, is dedicated to all the base event and listener classes.

Component provides an addListener method as a starting point for all events used within GXT, and also fires associated events based on the widget life cycle and state changes. Some widgets provide additional convenience methods for adding specific event listeners. You can also add these listeners by using Component's addListener method with the correct event type.

Tip   The list of events for each widget can be found in the Javadocs that show the events that will be fired by the widget's superclass.

All events extend BaseEvent and, depending on the type of event, support a setCancelled method that can be used to cancel an event and its associated action. As an example, if you add a listener for a window's BeforeHide event, when setCancelled(true) is set on the WindowEvent, the window's hide() call will be cancelled. The window will continue to show even though the user successfully clicked the close-window button that normally hides the window from view.

Sinking Events

In GWT, if you are creating a widget, you need to *sink* the events you are interested in receiving. There is a long and complex explanation for why this has been designed this way, but the short answer is, to avoid memory leaks.

As GXT is an extension of GWT, you need to sink events for widgets that don't have support for the events you are interested in. So if you want an Html widget to respond to mouse-over events, you need to sink the event before it starts receiving those browser events. As GXT doesn't attach to the DOM until after rendering, you need to sink events during (or after) the rendering process. Listing 3-1 shows the process for sinking all mouse events.

Listing 3-1. Sink Events

```
Html text = new Html("I will highlight on hover") {
  protected void onRender(Element target, int index) {
    super.onRender(target, index);
    el().addEventsSunk(Event.MOUSEEVENTS);
  }
};

Listener<BaseEvent> listener;
listener = new Listener<BaseEvent>() {
  public void handleEvent(BaseEvent be) {
    Html h = (Html) be.getSource();
    int b = h.el().getIntStyleAttribute("fontWeight");
    b = b == 900 ? 100 : 900;
    h.setIntStyleAttribute("fontWeight", b);
  }
};

text.addListener(Events.OnMouseOver, listener);
text.addListener(Events.OnMouseOut, listener);
text.setPagePosition(20, 20);
RootPanel.get().add(text);
```

In Listing 3-1, I first create an Html widget, and then using Java's inner class support, override the onRender method. After calling super, I grab an instance of the wrapped El to add the MOUSEEVENTS event to the element's existing sunk events.

Next, it's a simple case of creating and adding a listener that toggles between two font-weight styles and then adding the listener for both OnMouseOver and OnMouseOut.

Note   Even though the correct CSS property is font-weight, JavaScript requires all properties to be in CamelCase. This means that instead of using a hyphen to separate the parts of the identifier, you capitalize the first letter after where the hyphen would have been, which is why the style attribute is fontWeight.

Container

Containers are widgets that contain child components. Internally, containers handle the life-cycle needs of their children, creating, attaching, and detaching as needed. Containers also manage all positioning and size requirements for their children. Examples of widgets that are containers are ButtonBar, HtmlContainer, Menu, Portal, Table, TabPanel, ToolBar, and Tree.

LayoutContainer

LayoutContainer is the base container for GXT that other containers extend to inherit "automatic layout" capability. One of the core capabilities of LayoutContainer is its ability to use various layout managers that will size and position child widgets in different ways.

The default layout manager for LayoutContainer is FlowLayout, which provides a normal HTML flow (the first widget starts at the top left and each widget is then added downwards). A range of layout managers is available, and I'll cover them all in Chapter 4.

At this stage, I will simply introduce LayoutContainer. Listing 3-2 demonstrates how to create a container that contains a widget and attaches it to a GWT RootPanel.

Listing 3-2. LayoutContainer

```
LayoutContainer container = new LayoutContainer();
container.add(new Button("Click Me"));
container.setSize(300,300);
container.setBorders(true);
RootPanel.get().add(container);
container.layout();
```

Unless LayoutContainer is placed within an existing container (with an appropriate layout manager), you must size the container and call layout() to render its children, as I have done in Listing 3-2.

Tip   By default, LayoutContainer has no appearance; therefore, it is hard to determine visually where its boundaries exist. Enabling a LayoutContainer's borders using setBorders(true) can be very helpful, as the outline of the container shows when rendered. When you can see the borders, you can understand better how a layout is being rendered.

HorizontalPanel and VerticalPanel

HorizontalPanel and VerticalPanel provide built-in layout functionality using an internal HTML table. These containers are basically convenience classes to assist with simplifying the layout steps.

- **HorizontalPanel**: Lays out its children in a single row using TableRowLayout

- **VerticalPanel**: Lays out its children in a single column using TableLayout

In Listing 3-3, I've added a Label widget to the HorizontalPanel but also included a layout hint, known as layout data. This layout data hint for TableLayout is, not surprisingly, called

`TableData` and can inform the layout manager that you want to align the cell content a particular way. In this case, I will inform the layout manager to align the cell horizontally to the right.

Listing 3-3. HorizontalPanel

```
HorizontalPanel hp = new HorizontalPanel();
hp.setWidth(300);
hp.setTableWidth("100%");
hp.add(new Label("Aligned Center"));
TableData td = new TableData();
td.setHorizontalAlign(HorizontalAlignment.RIGHT);
hp.add(new Label("Aligned Right"), td);
RootPanel.get().add(hp);
```

Layout managers use layout data hints when the layout executes. These hints can provide additional size, margin, and position information about the child widget (just like Listing 3-3 uses `TableData` to advise the layout manager that the cell should align content to the right). You'll see more of these layout data hints as we progress, and we'll cover this concept further in Chapter 4.

ContentPanel

This container has functionality and structural components that make it the perfect building block for application-oriented user interfaces. It contains button bars, support for top and bottom components, and separate header, footer, and body sections. The panel's header supports an icon, text, and buttons. The panel's body can be expanded and collapsed.

ContentPanel, like LayoutContainer, needs to be sized unless it is placed into a container with an appropriate layout. An example ContentPanel container is shown in Figure 3-3.

Figure 3-3. ContentPanel example

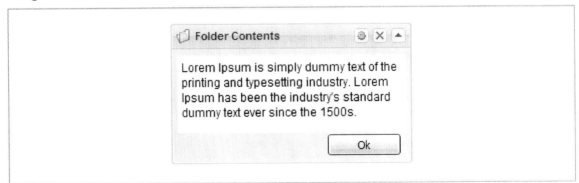

To get the body text of the ContentPanel to look just like Figure 3-3, I need to add a few styles to our application's web page. If you're using the MyApp example created in Chapter 2, then edit the MyApp.css file located along with your HTML file. The GWT webAppCreator tool created this file, and it will be full of GWT-specific content. Since we won't be using any of the existing content, remove all lines so the file is empty.

Add the following lines, and ensure your MyApp.css file looks similar. We'll continue to add content to this CSS file in Chapter 6, when we implement a full application example.

```
* {
  font-family: arial, helvetica, tahoma, sans-serif;
}

.text {
  font-size: 12px;
}
```

The first style sets all styles to use the font families found in the order I've specified. The second style sets the size of text to 12 point.

Apart from adding style information within a CSS resource file, you can also add style information directly to certain aspects of the rendered widget. Listing 3-4 demonstrates both methods.

Listing 3-4. ContentPanel

```
ContentPanel cp = new ContentPanel();
cp.setHeading("Folder Contents");
cp.setBounds(10, 10, 250, 140);
cp.setCollapsible(true);
cp.setFrame(true);
cp.setBodyStyle("backgroundColor: white;");
cp.getHeader().addTool(new ToolButton("x-tool-gear"));
cp.getHeader().addTool(new ToolButton("x-tool-close"));
cp.addText(getBogusText());
cp.addButton(new Button("Ok"));
cp.setIconStyle("tree-folder-open");
RootPanel.get().add(cp);
cp.layout();
```

Tip   While it is generally bad practice to embed style information within GWT source code, if you do wish to temporarily do this, remember this tip: all CSS properties must be in CamelCase. For example, "background-color: white" needs to be "backgroundColor: white".

There are quite a few new concepts in this Listing 3-4. Here is a quick outline of the methods used and what they do:

- setHeading: Sets the title of the panel's heading.

- setCollapsible: Enables/disables the collapsible feature and the associated header icon. This can also be used with setAnimCollapse to control the animated slide-in/out effect.

- setFrame: Enables/disables a rendering effect of custom rounded borders and a colored background. Otherwise, borders are square and 1 pixel in width.

- setBodyStyle: Allows you to specify CSS style information for the internal body section of the panel. All attributes must be in lower camel case.

- getHeader().addTool: Allows you to modify the panel's header to add prebuilt or custom tool items. I'll provide more detail on tool buttons later in the chapter.

- addText: A convenience method that creates an Html widget and adds it to the panel. You can insert any valid HTML fragment.

- addButton: Another convenience method that adds a button to a button bar located within the footer of the panel.

- setIconStyle: Lets you provide an image that will be rendered as part of the panel's header icon. The icon style is a CSS element that essentially contains the URL location of the image file. In Listing 3-4, I grabbed the icon style from the GXT library.

DO I NEED TO MESS WITH CSS?

You might be wondering if you need to know a lot about CSS or if you can build a web application without having to know much at all about web styles.

While it is not mandatory to delve deeply into CSS with GXT, if you do customize some style elements, you can get some neat results. For example, you can provide subtle adjustments to color, size, padding, or margins that improve the visual aspect of your rich Internet application.

Ultimately, how much you focus on custom styles is up to you. At the extreme end, you can even build your own custom theme containing styles and images tailored to suit your organization's own look and feel.

Viewport

Viewport is a LayoutContainer that fills the browser's window and monitors window resizing. When the browser window is resized, Viewport executes its layout, causing children to resize and adjust to the new window dimensions. Listing 3-5 shows Viewport's syntax.

Listing 3-5. Viewport

```
Viewport viewport = new Viewport();
viewport.add(new ContentPanel(), new MarginData(10));
RootPanel.get().add(viewport);
```

As Viewport extends LayoutContainer, and therefore inherits LayoutContainer's functionality, you will notice the use of another layout data hint, MarginData, which informs the layout to add a 10-pixel margin to the ContentPanel.

Unlike LayoutContainer, Viewport automatically executes its layout when the application is started. You simply add Viewport to RootPanel, and Viewport handles the rest. As such, Viewport is often used as the topmost widget when building an application that can adjust to various window sizes.

Window and Dialog

The Window widget provides a floating container that offers similar functionality to windows you would find in standard desktop user interfaces. Windows can be modal, shown and hidden, and maximized and restored. As it extends ContentPanel, Window offers all the same visual and functional features found in ContentPanel.

Unlike ContentPanel, you don't add Window to a Container (or RootPanel). When Window's show() method is called, Window adds itself to the DOM, sets its z-index to be the topmost item, and makes itself visible. At this time, Window also executes its layout and centers itself within the current view.

If you intend to reuse Window, you should hide instead of close it, as closing releases all resources and requires you to re-create the Window if you need to show it again. Listing 3-6 shows Window's syntax.

Listing 3-6. Window

```
Window w = new Window();
w.setHeading("Product Information");
w.setModal(true);
w.setSize(600, 400);
w.setMaximizable(true);
w.setToolTip("The GXT product page...");
w.setUrl("http://www.extjs.com/products/gxt");
w.show();
```

In Listing 3-6, you'll notice the use of the setUrl method, which adds an IFrame and displays content from the specified URL. The GWT hosted shell will alert you to a security risk, which is a result of the content coming from outside the hosted shell's environment.

Dialog simply extends Window and adds support for buttons and a few extra convenience methods for handling them. You would typically use Dialog as a convenient way to build a window with OK/Cancel/Yes/No buttons. Listing 3-7 demonstrates the use of buttons and the optional HideOnButtonClick method, which hides the dialog after the user clicks the button.

Listing 3-7. Dialog

```
Dialog d = new Dialog();
d.setHeading("Exit Warning!");
d.addText("Do you wish to save before exiting?");
d.setBodyStyle("fontSize:14px;fontWeight:bold;padding:13px;");
d.setSize(300, 120);
d.setHideOnButtonClick(true);
d.setButtons(Dialog.YESNOCANCEL);
d.show();
```

The setButtons convenience method in Listing 3-7 provides a quick way to create a dialog with Yes, No, and Cancel buttons added and positioned correctly.

Also, note the body styles that ensure the text weight is bold and the body padding is set to 13 pixels. In this example, it's fairly straightforward to embed the styles in code, but in a real production project you should consider adding this style information via CSS files to make it easier to change and adjust styles without having to recompile your project.

MessageBox

A MessageBox component is similar in behavior to JavaScript's window.alert() in that it pops up a modal dialog, an associated icon, and a message requesting user input. Fundamentally, MessageBox is a convenience class that builds and manipulates a Dialog component in a defined way.

You saw an example of MessageBox in Chapter 2, and its use is fairly straightforward. One of the interesting aspects of MessageBox (and this is no different than Window or Dialog) is that it doesn't halt JavaScript program execution, unlike JavaScript's window.alert(), which does. This provides some nice benefits and some potential pitfalls if you don't consider the implication of the nonblocking nature of Window and Dialog.

Because there is no halt to code execution, a common question is how to create the prompt "Are you sure?" when a Window is closing. The solution is quite ingenious: use Event. setCancelled(true) to stop the window from hiding, and then show the MessageBox. If the user clicks Yes and wishes to continue to hide the window, I simply remove the listener that would set setCancelled(true) against the event (and stop the hide), and then call Window.hide() again. The hide won't be stopped because the listener was removed.

Listing 3-8 demonstrates this solution, along with a typical use of MessageBox using the confirm method to ask the user "Are you sure?".

Listing 3-8. Window Close, AreYouSure?

```
final Window w = new Window();
w.setHeading("Close me...");
w.setSize(300, 200);
Listener wL = new Listener() {
  public void handleEvent(BaseEvent be) {
    be.setCancelled(true);
    Listener<MessageBoxEvent> cb;
    cb = new Listener<MessageBoxEvent>() {
      public void handleEvent(MessageBoxEvent mbe) {
        String id = mbe.getButtonClicked().getItemId();
        if (Dialog.YES == id) {
          w.removeAllListeners();
          w.hide();
        }
      }
    };
    MessageBox.confirm("Close?", "Are you sure?", cb);
  }
};
w.addListener(Events.BeforeHide, wL);
w.show();
```

In addition to confirm, MessageBox also has alert, which displays a single OK button and a read-only message alerting the user, and prompt, which provides a text field for user input along with OK and Cancel buttons. Optionally, you can also show a multiline prompt that uses a text field to obtain more than a single line of text from the user.

TabPanel and TabItem

A tabbed panel is now a popular user interface used within browsers. It allows different content to be seen on the main viewing panel as each tab is selected. TabPanel is a container of TabItems, and both are used together to achieve the same effect. An example TabPanel with TabItems is shown in Figure 3-4.

Figure 3-4. TabPanel example

TabPanel can be configured with tabs at the top or bottom. When showing tabs on the top, you can also set setEnableTabScroll to true. If more tabs exist than can be shown, TabPanel will automatically scroll the tab header left or right as more tabs are added or removed.

Each TabItem supports a display icon and an optional Close button that removes the tab from the panel when the user clicks it. TabItems can also be disabled. Listing 3-9 shows the TabPanel and TabItem syntax.

Listing 3-9. TabPanel and TabItem

```
TabPanel tp = new TabPanel();
TabItem pti = new TabItem("Project");
pti.setIconStyle("tree-folder-open");
tp.add(pti);
tp.add(new TabItem("TabPanel.java"));
TabItem ti = new TabItem("TabItem.java");
ti.setClosable(true);
ti.setEnabled(false);
tp.add(ti);
tp.setBounds(10, 10, 300, 300);
RootPanel.get().add(tp);
```

Html and HtmlContainer

The Html widget allows you to inject HTML fragments. Using Html, you can inject HTML wrapped in a tag of your choosing, or <div> if you don't specify one. Listing 3-10 shows a few simple HTML tags with text being added directly to RootPanel.

Listing 3-10. Html

```
Html h = new Html(
  "<div class=text style='padding:5px'>"
  + "<h1>Heading1</h1>"
  + "<i>Some text</i></br>"
  + "Some more text</br>"
  + "<u>Final text</u></div>");
RootPanel.get().add(h);
```

HtmlContainer provides a widget for HTML fragments, but wraps this functionality in a container. Additionally, HtmlContainer supports loading HTML fragments from a URL or a GWT RequestBuilder, as well as a supplied String. HtmlContainer also allows you to add other widgets into the container by using a selector. Selectors are used to select elements in the HTML. The selected elements are then used as targets for inserting the widget.

The following code snippet is the Fragment.html used in Listing 3-11. You'll notice it contains a td element with an ID of widget1.

```
<table>
  <tr>
    <td>This is a test.</td>
  </tr>
  <tr>
    <td id="widget1">This content is replaced.</td>
  </tr>
</table>
```

In Listing 3-11, a button is added to the container using that ID to target the insertion.

Listing 3-11. HtmlContainer

```
HtmlContainer hc = new HtmlContainer();
hc.setUrl("Fragment.html");
hc.setBorders(true);
hc.setBounds(10, 10, 200, 100);
Button button = new Button("Click Me");
hc.add(button, "#widget1");
RootPanel.get().add(container);
```

Note   When using Html or HtmlContainer, ensure that correct style information is being used. HTML fragments are subject to the same style information as everything else, and that might not always be what you want. In other words, you may need to apply specific styles to your HTML fragments so that you avoid the general styles being applied from the `ext-all.css` file.

ProgressBar

ProgressBars are a neat way to show progress when the user is waiting for some lengthy operation to complete. A progress bar gives the user feedback about the operation still occurring or how much further the operation will take to complete by showing a bar that progressively grows from left to right as it updates.

There are two methods for using a progress bar. The first is when information is available to show how much the operation has changed, and therefore the progress bar status can update at various points in time. The second is when update information is not available to show, and so the progress bar auto-updates continuously by itself. Listing 3-13 demonstrates the first method, as it's a little more involved, and some GWT timer code as well.

Listing 3-13. ProgressBar

```
final ProgressBar bar = new ProgressBar();
bar.setBounds(10, 10, 200, Style.DEFAULT);
Timer t = new Timer() {
  int val = 0;

  public void run() {
    if (val == 10) {
      bar.updateProgress(1, "Completed");
    } else {
      val++;
      String status = (val * 10) + "% Complete"
      status +=" (Task " + val / 2 + " of 5)";
      bar.updateProgress(val / 10.0, status);
      this.schedule(500);
    }
  }
};
t.schedule(1000);
RootPanel.get().add(bar);
```

Listing 3-13 utilizes the GWT Timer class, which is set to run first in 1,000 ms and then to execute every 500 ms. When the run() method is executed by Timer, it checks to see if val has reached 10. If not, the method increments val and then builds a string to display within the progress bar. Finally, the updateProgress method is called with a percentage value, and the display string and timer are scheduled to run again.

You'll notice that updateProgress requires a double value less than 1.0 to reflect the percentage of the progress bar to be shown (0.0 equals 0% and shows no bar, and 1.0 equals 100% and shows the entire bar).

Tip　　　In Listing 3-13, we sized and positioned the progress bar using setBounds, and set the Style.DEFAULT for the height of the widget. This default value can be applied to any widget to allow natural sizing.

Slider

Another neat way to manipulate data is with the Slider widget. Slider is best used when you need the user to adjust the value of some item between a range of values—much simpler than entering values or selecting from a list. Slider, shown in Figure 3-5, is a natural user control for quickly adjusting values.

Figure 3-5. Slider example

Slider is very simple to use. Set up the minimum and maximum values, the increment amount and starting value, and optionally a tool tip–styled message. The message string will replace the {0} parameter with the current value of the slider.

Listing 3-14 puts this into action.

Listing 3-14. Slider

```
Slider slider = new Slider();
slider.setBounds(10, 10, 200, Style.DEFAULT);
slider.setMinValue(1);
slider.setMaxValue(100);
slider.setIncrement(1);
slider.setValue(100);
slider.setMessage("Scale by {0}%");
RootPanel.get().add(slider);
```

DataList

DataList is a simple list with the capability to render text or HTML fragments as list items.
DataList also supports icons and individual styles. Listing 3-15 displays the same information as
Listing 3-16, but you'll notice in Listing 3-15 that the data and rendering information are
combined within the list item text.

Listing 3-15. DataList

```
DataList dl = new DataList();
dl.add("<b>SAAB</b> 9000 <i>(1994)</i>");
dl.add("<b>BMW</b> 318i <i>(1999)</i>");
dl.add("<b>VW</b> Golf <i>(2001)</i>");
dl.add("<b>Peugeot</b> 307 <i>(2002)</i>");
dl.setBounds(10, 10, 160,60);
RootPanel.get().add(dl);
Listener listener = new Listener<DataListEvent>(){
  public void handleEvent(DataListEvent be) {
    DataListItem dli = be.getSelected().get(0);
    System.out.println(dli.getText());
  }
};
dl.addListener(Events.SelectionChange, listener);
```

A range of events is also fired relating to the selection and list modification, such as
add/remove. You listen for events by simply adding a Listener to DataList. All events fire a
DataListEvent and assign values to the appropriate fields, depending on the event. The Javadoc
for each event outlines this behavior.

Using DataList is very straightforward. There are no complex data setup requirements
compared to ListView (which is explained in the next section). While DataList is simpler, it has
the disadvantage of not really keeping the data and the view separated. For simple lists, this
isn't an issue, but for more advanced list rendering, consider using ListView.

ListView

ListView is the first widget that utilizes the Store and Data packages. These utility packages are used to assist in the local caching and representation of data models. These models are then used by the view widgets (like ListView, Grid, etc.) to render and display data. I will go into a lot more detail regarding the Store and Data APIs in Chapter 5.

In Listing 3-16, CarModel is a ModelData class that holds our car information. This class is used by the widgets that use ModelData classes (BaseModel is derived from ModelData). Notice the calls to set(name,value), which use a property name to identify the field and a value to store the data. In Figure 3-6 and Listing 3-16, I use the property names car_make, car_model, and car_year. I'll also use this CarModel class throughout the book.

Listing 3-16. CarModel

```
public class CarModel extends BaseModel implements Serializable {
    private static final long serialVersionUID = 1L;
    public CarModel(String mk, String ml, Integer y) {
        set("car_make", mk);
        set("car_model", ml);
        set("car_year", y);
    }
}
```

As Figure 3-6 shows, ListView is a widget that is really handy for displaying a list of styled data, similar to DataList, except that you can customize the style and rendering information independently from the data. In ListView, your data models and rendering styles are defined separately.

Figure 3-6. ListView example

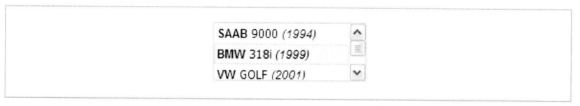

ListView offers this capability through the use of a powerful templating system called XTemplates. XTemplates provides an advanced way of rendering HTML and style information that is closely coupled with data. I'll cover XTemplates in Chapter 4.

Listing 3-17 uses the convenience method setSimpleTemplate, which requires you to list the data element names surrounded by the HTML you wish to render per line. Under the hood, this method uses an XTemplate, but allows you to avoid having to know how it works for simple examples.

Listing 3-17. ListView

```
ListStore<CarModel> store = new ListStore<CarModel>();
store.add(new CarModel("SAAB","9000",1994));
store.add(new CarModel("BMW","318i",1999));
store.add(new CarModel("VW","GOLF",2001));
store.add(new CarModel("Peugeot","307",2002));
ListView<CarModel> lv = new ListView<CarModel>();
lv.setStore(store);
lv.setSimpleTemplate(
  "<b>{car_make}</b> {car_model} <i>({car_year})</i>");
lv.setBounds(10, 10, 160,60);
RootPanel.get().add(lv);
```

.widget.button

Buttons are a fundamental user control of any user application and, as you'd expect, GXT has solid support in this area. In this section I'll cover the Button class and the various button containers.

Buttons can be styled in numerous ways in any combination of the following:

- **Scale**: Support for small, medium, and large button styles

- **Icon**: Can be positioned either left, right, top, or bottom

- **Arrow**: Can be added to the right or on the bottom

Extended versions of Button, such as ToggleButton and SplitButton, provide additional functionality. Figure 3-7 shows an example of the three scale sizes of SplitButton.

Figure 3-7. SplitButton example

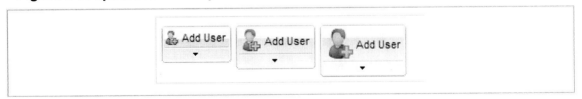

Button, ToggleButton, and SplitButton

Button is a fairly obvious widget that doesn't need explanation.

ToggleButton, like its namesake, is a button that can toggle its pushed state on and off. Think of ToggleButton as similar to the Bold or Italic buttons shown in most rich text editors.

SplitButton, also like its namesake, is a button that has a split with an arrow (as shown in Figure 3-7) that can be clicked independently of the base button; normally, a contextual pop-up menu shows. A common example is color pickers that show a selected color and then a pop-up color table when the user clicks the split arrow.

All buttons have the ability to enable and disable, the ability to modify their displayed text, and a method to set an icon to be displayed with or instead of text. As expected, you can add event listeners to handle selection events. Listing 3-18 shows a "Click Me" button with an icon and responds to events by showing a JavaScript alert when clicked.

Listing 3-18. Button

```
Button button = new Button("Click Me");
button.setIconStyle("my-icon");
button.setEnabled(true);
SelectionListener<ComponentEvent> sl = new
  SelectionListener<ComponentEvent>(){
  public void componentSelected(ComponentEvent ce) {
    Window.alert("clicked");
  }};
button.addSelectionListener(sl);
RootPanel.get().add(button);
RootPanel.get().add(new ToggleButton("Bold"));
```

In Listing 3-18, I added a custom icon by setting the icon style to my-icon. This style name is defined in our application's MyApp.css file.

The required format for an icon style is as follows:

```
.my-icon { background: url(images/icons/my-icon.png
) no-repeat center left !important; }
```

Status

The Status widget is essentially a BoxComponent with the appropriate styling enabled to show an indented box border or an animated rotating icon. These provide a range of status styles for various purposes.

Status can be combined with ToolBar (introduced later in the chapter) to produce a typical-looking status bar. Another common use of Status is to wrap it in a ButtonAdapter and add it to the button bar of a ContentPanel. Used as a "please wait, I'm working" indicator, Status's setBusy method adds an icon along with the status text.

Both of these approaches are shown in Figure 3-8.

Figure 3-8. Status example

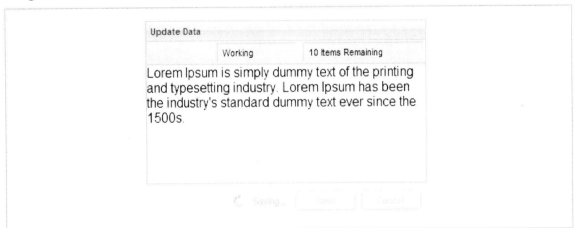

Listing 3-19 pulls together a few concepts already covered into a nice example.

Listing 3-19. Status

```
final ContentPanel cp = new ContentPanel();
cp.setHeading("Update Data");
cp.setBounds(10, 10, 350, 240);
cp.setButtonAlign(HorizontalAlignment.RIGHT);
cp.addText(CodeSnippet.DUMMY_TEXT_SHORT);

ToolBar topStatus = new ToolBar();
topStatus.add(new FillToolItem());

Status working = new Status();
working.setWidth(100);
working.setText("Working");
working.setBox(true);
topStatus.add(working);
topStatus.add(new LabelToolItem(" "));
Status remaining = new Status();
remaining.setWidth(150);
remaining.setText("10 Items Remaining");
remaining.setBox(true);
topStatus.add(remaining);
cp.setTopComponent(topStatus);

final Status saving = new Status();
saving.setBusy("Saving...");
saving.hide();
saving.setAutoWidth(true);

Button button = new Button("Save");
cp.addButton(new ButtonAdapter(saving));
cp.addButton(button);
cp.addButton(new Button("Cancel"));
RootPanel.get().add(cp);

SelectionListener<ButtonEvent> sl
= new SelectionListener<ButtonEvent>() {
  public void componentSelected(ButtonEvent be) {
    cp.getButtonBar().setEnabled(false);
    saving.show();
  }
};
button.addSelectionListener(sl);
```

IconButton and ToolButton

IconButtons are used where you need a small visual button that doesn't require a text explanation of what the button action does. Common examples are the close or minimize buttons on windows. If you wish, you can define your own IconButton, but you'll need to include the icon image and two other icons that represent the hover-over and disabled styles. The hover-over and disabled style names are set by adding the text -over and -disabled to the defined base style name.

GXT includes a range of predefined icons in the ToolButton widget. Figure 3-9 illustrates all of the available ToolButton options, placed onto a ContentPanel's header.

Figure 3-9. ToolButton example

.widget.toolbar

This section outlines the .toolbar package and its associated classes. Toolbars offer a wider selection of widgets than what simple IconButtons can offer. With a toolbar, you can basically add any widget you like, as shown in Figure 3-10.

Figure 3-10. ToolBar example

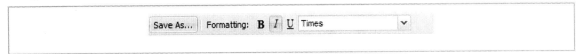

The ToolBar is also a widget that can exist on its own, without needing to be part of a ContentPanel. In Listing 3-20, I've added a ToolBar directly to the browser's RootPanel, and it correctly sizes itself to fill the width of the window.

Listing 3-20. ToolBar

```
ToolBar tb = new ToolBar();
tb.add(new Button("Save As..."));
tb.add(new SeparatorToolItem());
tb.add(new LabelToolItem("Formatting:"));
String txt = "<span style='font:bold 14px times'>B</span>";
tb.add(new ToggleButton(txt));
txt = "<span style='font:italic 14px times'>I</span>";
tb.add(new ToggleButton(txt));
```

```
txt = "<span style='font:14px times"
+ ";text-decoration:underline'>U</span>";
tb.add(new ToggleButton(txt));
SimpleComboBox<String> scb = new SimpleComboBox<String>();
scb.add("Arial");
scb.add("Courier");
scb.add("Times");
tb.add(scb);
RootPanel.get().add(tb);
```

You'll notice that I've also added a SimpleComboBox to the toolbar by wrapping it in an AdapterToolItem. You can do this with any object that extends com.google.gwt.user.client.ui.Widget, which includes all of the GXT widgets.

Note   I will be covering ComboBox when we get to the section on forms, so don't be too concerned about how SimpleComboBox works.

.widget.menu

The classes within the .widget.menu package provide support for traditional menu bars and menu items, and allow you to build comprehensive menus and submenus like the example in Figure 3-11.

Figure 3-11. Menu example

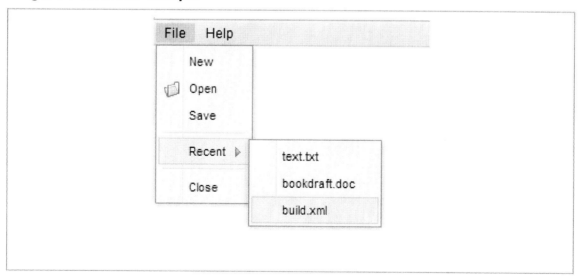

The Menu and MenuItem classes provide the majority of the functionality. A few additional classes add specific features like a separator line, support for check boxes against menu items, and a date menu item for selecting dates.

A menu can be added to most widgets, and in Figure 3-11, the menu was added to a MenuBar. Logically, menus are a hierarchical list of items, and building them is performed in a similar way: you hierarchically create the list of items and submenu items. When a submenu is needed, you create another menu, which also has menu items, and so on.

Listing 3-21 outlines the MenuBar building hierarchy.

Listing 3-21. MenuBar

```
Menu fileMenu = new Menu();
fileMenu.add(new MenuItem("New"));
fileMenu.add(new MenuItem("Open", "tree-folder-open"));
fileMenu.add(new MenuItem("Save"));

fileMenu.add(new SeparatorMenuItem());

MenuItem sub = new MenuItem("Recent");
Menu recent = new Menu();
recent.add(new MenuItem("text.txt"));
recent.add(new MenuItem("bookdraft.doc"));
recent.add(new MenuItem("build.xml"));
sub.setSubMenu(recent);
fileMenu.add(sub);

fileMenu.add(new SeparatorMenuItem());
fileMenu.add(new MenuItem("Close"));

Menu helpMenu = new Menu();
helpMenu.add(new MenuItem("Help Topics"));
helpMenu.add(new SeparatorMenuItem());
helpMenu.add(new MenuItem("About"));

MenuBar mb = new MenuBar();
mb.add(new MenuBarItem("File",fileMenu));
mb.add(new MenuBarItem("Help",helpMenu));

RootPanel.get().add(mb);
```

Menus can be added to widgets that have a setMenu(Menu) method. When selected, these widgets show the menu. Other widgets have a setContextMenu(Menu) method, and show the menu when it is right-clicked.

.widget.tips

ToolTips, when added to widgets, provide additional information about the widget when you hover over the widget, as illustrated in Figure 3-12.

Figure 3-12. ToolTip example

All widgets that extend Component include support for a setToolTip(String) method as a convenient way to quickly set up a tool tip. In addition, Component provides a setToolTip(ToolTipConfig) method that adds further tool tip configuration flexibility as well as a convenience method for adding tool tips.

Listing 3-22 illustrates both of these methods of adding tool tips to some buttons.

Listing 3-22. ToolTip

```
HorizontalPanel hp = new HorizontalPanel();
hp.setSpacing(20);
Button b1 = new Button("Inject");
b1.setToolTip("Inject the web with cool applications.");
Button b2 = new Button("Extract");
ToolTipConfig ttc = new ToolTipConfig();
ttc.setTitle("Major Extraction Process");
ttc.setText("Begin the extensive extraction process
 that will get all knowledge from the Internet.");
b2.setToolTip(ttc);
hp.add(b1);
hp.add(b2);
RootPanel.get().add(hp);
```

Another option for adding tool tips is QuickTip. QuickTip extends ToolTip and obtains its configuration information directly through markup. Using the element attributes, QuickTip provides a quick solution to adding tool tips when you're using templates or specifying the HTML markup directly.

QuickTip supports the following attributes:

- qtip: The tool tip message (required)
- qtitle: The title of the tool tip (optional)
- qwidth: The width of the toot tip (optional)

Listing 3-23 adds a QuickTip to an Html widget.

Listing 3-23. QuickTip

```
String qtip = "We're in the business of big things!!";
String qtitle = "About Us...";
String text = "Big Business Enterprises";

Html h = new Html("<div qtip=\"" + qtip
    + "\" qtitle=\"" + qtitle + "\" qwidth=120>"
    + text + "</div>");
h.setIntStyleAttribute("fontWeight", 700);
new QuickTip(h);

RootPanel.get().add(h);
```

State Management

Often when building a web application, you'd like to save some user setting or attribute based on information such as the user's last setting, which tab they had open, or the check boxes they last clicked. Rather than persisting this information to a database, you can use cookies to store this information locally within the browser.

The GXT com.extjs.gxt.ui.client.state.StateManager class performs this task fairly easily. The default implementation of StateManager uses GWT client-side cookies to store all state information (via a simple CookieProvider implementation). The Provider class takes care of the initialization and transformation of data into and out of cookies.

You use the StateManager as follows:

```
StateManager.get().set("id", obj);
```

where id is the identification tag and obj is any kind of object data you wish to store.

In GXT, you can also store state data within every widget that extends Component—and that's all of them. Component's getState() method returns a Map that you can use to store any number of objects and data. When you have completed storing or updating objects, you then call saveState() to ensure all data is stored away using the persistence method within the current StateManager instance.

Themes—Let's Make It Pretty

Themes within GXT provide an extensible way to visually change the look of all the included widgets. There are three built-in themes: *Blue* (the default), *Gray*, and *Slate*. Each theme includes all the CSS and images needed to uniquely style and render the widgets correctly for each supported browser.

> ## USING OTHER THEMES
>
> In addition to the provided themes, the GXT community has also published a range of themes. Many of the Ext JS framework themes can also be adapted to work with GXT. All that is required is to extend the class theme and create a constructor that calls the superclass with a static name and the required CSS file. You'll also need to include the CSS and all the associated images so they can be located.

While Blue is the default theme for all GXT applications, it is possible to change to a different theme. For example, to make the Gray theme the default, use the following line:

```
GXT.setDefaultTheme(Theme.GRAY, true);
```

This needs to be the very first thing your application does. This is important because all widgets extend the GXT Component class, and Component statically calls GXT.init() when instantiated, and so will enable the default theme, all before you can change it to something else.

Note   This is an important concept to understand: something as simple as your application's main entry point class extending LayoutContainer will result in GXT.init() being executed before you can change the default theme.

The solution is to ensure your application's main entry point class simply implements com.google.gwt.core.client.EntryPoint and does not statically or otherwise instantiate any GXT classes before you change the default theme.

The other included theme, Slate, is only defined differently as an example of a custom theme. Slate essentially provides a model on which you can create and extend your own theme, or include one of the existing Ext JS community themes. As the Slate theme is a custom theme, it must be registered with the ThemeManager, which is performed as follows:

```
ThemeManager.register(Slate.SLATE);
```

Figure 3-13 shows an example of a ContentPanel and a few widgets using the Slate theme.

Figure 3-13. Slate theme example

GXT also provides a widget that simplifies the user theme selection and change process. ThemeSelector is a drop-down selection box with the necessary code to display the current theme. When the selection changes, the theme switches by reloading the application.

Listing 3-24 builds the Slate theme example.

Listing 3-24. QuickTip

```
GXT.setDefaultTheme(Slate.SLATE, false);
ThemeManager.register(Slate.SLATE);

ContentPanel cp = new ContentPanel();
cp.setHeading("Themes...");
cp.setBounds(10, 10, 250, 140);
cp.setCollapsible(true);
cp.setFrame(true);
cp.addText("The current theme is : "+GXT.getThemeId());
cp.add(new ThemeSelector());
cp.addButton(new Button("OK"));
RootPanel.get().add(cp);
cp.layout();

StateManager.get().set(GWT.getModuleBaseURL() + "theme", "");
```

Note that in Listing 3-24, GXT.setDefaultTheme is called with the second parameter (force) set to false. When GXT initializes, it interrogates a local browser cookie to determine the previous default theme. Setting force to true will override the previous theme, whereas false will only change the default theme if no previous theme has been saved.

The last line in Listing 3-24 clears this theme cookie. You may wish to do this when you are testing and verifying how things work when using themes and defaults.

Summary

At this stage in the book, you should be really getting a good handle on the range of widgets and possibilities with GXT. I've covered the basics of a GXT application by covering how things are rendered and providing an overview of the event system, which led into an explanation of the Container classes, such as ViewPort, LayoutContainer, ContentPanel, and TabPanel, and the Window, Dialog, and MessageBox widgets.

I then moved onto some more widgets, such as Html and ProgressBar; introduced the first of the data widgets, DataList and ListView; and finally discussed the Button, ToolBar, Menu, and Tips widgets.

Wow! This certainly has been a weighty chapter with plenty of coverage. The next chapter steps it up again and explains how layouts work in GXT, introduces the range of layout managers, begins the coverage on some of the advanced stuff (such as Forms, Portal, and Drag-n-Drop), and shows you how to use XTemplates.

Chapter 4: Advanced Widgets and Stuff

Let's turn up the gas and jump into some more advanced (and exciting) features of GXT: Layouts, Forms, Portal, and Drag-n-Drop.

Layout managers are probably one of the most important features of GXT to learn. As layout managers translate code into a visual arrangement of widgets, it is critical that you provide the correct instructions and hints so that GXT can position and size widgets in the places you intended.

Forms and their associated widgets are a fundamental part of any application, and so GXT has a good helping of Form widgets and components to make your applications look very tasty.

Portal and Drag-n-Drop round out the coverage of the advanced stuff in this chapter. Portal allows you to build an application that has iGoogle-like panel Portlets. The Drag-n-Drop API allows you to add drag-and-drop functionality to widgets that support it.

Layouts

In the previous chapter, I introduced the concept of layout managers. A fundamental part of GXT containers, layout managers are designed to assist in the positioning and sizing of child widgets. Layout managers perform an important function in creating a consistent user interface for applications rendered using the browser's inherent HTML layout capabilities.

GWT Panels

Before we introduce GXT layout managers, it is helpful to understand how GWT performs its layouts. In GWT, panels themselves are responsible for creating the required markup and inserting their children into the DOM.

To make this clearer, let's go through a GWT example. Consider what happens when the GWT compiler executes this bit of code:

```
VerticalPanel panel = new VerticalPanel();
```

Upon executing this single line, GWT immediately generates this markup in the DOM:

```
<TABLE cellSpacing=0 cellPadding=0>
<TBODY>
</TBODY>
</TABLE>
```

If we now add a child to the panel, the panel generates further markup and inserts this item in the DOM. Let's add a label to the panel as follows:

```
VerticalPanel panel = new VerticalPanel();
panel.add(new Label("Child 1"));
```

This results in the following markup:

```
<TABLE cellSpacing=0 cellPadding=0>
 <TBODY>
  <TR>
   <TD style="VERTICAL-ALIGN: top" align=left>
     <DIV class=gwt-Label>Child 1</DIV>
   </TD>
  </TR>
 </TBODY>
</TABLE>
```

The pattern here is that GWT will insert and manipulate the structure of the DOM as each child is added to the panel. If we remove the label from the panel, the table row will be immediately removed.

Unlike GWT panels, containers in GXT do not physically connect child components to the container's DOM. This task is taken care of by layout managers.

Replicating the previous GWT example, let's begin by creating a container with a vertical layout that utilizes a table structure.

```
LayoutContainer container = new LayoutContainer();
container.setLayout(new TableLayout(1)); // 1 column
```

At this point, no HTML elements have been created. This is quite different from GWT panels that would have already generated HTML elements for the panel and its children. Going further, let's add a child label:

```
LayoutContainer container = new LayoutContainer();
container.setLayout(new TableLayout(1)); // 1 column
container.add(new Label("Child 1"));
```

Even after adding a child component, no HTML elements have been created. You might now be wondering, "So when do the elements get created?"

Excellent question! In order for the container's HTML to be created and children inserted, the container's layout must execute. There are several ways in which the layout can execute, but for now, let's go with the simplest case in which the layout executes, when the container is *attached*. Attached is a GWT term that indicates that the widget is part of the browser's DOM. Attaching and detaching are subjects on their own, so let's assume they mean when the widget is added to and removed from the page.

When we add the container to RootPanel, the container will be attached, and the container's layout will execute. Let's now add that final bit of code to the example.

```
LayoutContainer container = new LayoutContainer();
container.setLayout(new TableLayout(1)); // 1 column
container.add(new Label("Child 1"));
RootPanel.get().add(container);
```

TableLayout executes, creates the container HTML structure, and inserts each child into its table cell. The resulting markup is as follows:

```
<div id="x-auto-0" style="overflow: hidden;">
 <table>
  <tbody>
   <tr>
    <td>
     <div id="x-auto-1" class="gwt-Label">Child 1</div>
    </td>
   </tr>
  </tbody>
 </table>
</div>
```

If GXT layout managers execute only when attached, what do we do when we add a child component after a container has attached? Let's add another child label to the container.

```
LayoutContainer container = new LayoutContainer();
container.setLayout(new TableLayout(1)); // 1 column
container.add(new Label("Child 1"));
RootPanel.get().add(container);
container.add(new Label("Child 2"));
```

As expected, the resulting HTML is exactly as before, because the layout manager executed when the container was attached. If we leave the example like this, the extra child will never be rendered.

The addition of the second child component requires that the layout be manually executed, and we do this by calling layout(), as follows:

```
LayoutContainer container = new LayoutContainer();
container.setLayout(new TableLayout(1)); // 1 column
container.add(new Label("Child 1"));
RootPanel.get().add(container);
container.add(new Label("Child 2"));
container.layout();
```

Manually executing the layout is required when the container has been attached (rendered), and you add child components.

Cascading Layouts

Previously, we discussed two ways of executing a container's layout. First, when the layout is executed as the container is attached; and second, when you call `layout()` manually on the container. There are other ways in which a layout can execute that relate to cascading containers and layouts.

After a container executes its layout, it determines if any of its children are containers. When it finds a child container, it then executes that child container's layout. So as long as there is a chain of containers, the execution of layouts will cascade to the child containers.

Note   Due to this cascading effect, you can lay out a top-level container and the child containers will adjust their layouts as well.

A container's layout will also execute when its size is adjusted. This is a default behavior and can be disabled. This means that if a container's size is changed, the layout (and any child container's layout managers) will update based on the container's new size.

Layout Managers

There are 16 layout managers available. Table 4-1 lists all the layout managers along with a short description and the purpose of each.

Table 4-1. The List of Available Layout Managers

LAYOUT MANAGER	DESCRIPTION / PURPOSE
AccordionLayout	This is a layout that contains multiple ContentPanels in an expandable accordion style such that only one panel can be open at any given time. Closed panels are shown as minimal title bar tabs placed above or below the currently open panel.
AnchorLayout	A layout that enables anchoring of contained widgets relative to the container's dimensions. For example, using this layout, you can specifiy that the widget takes up 50 percent of the container's width and 100 percent of its height.

Table 4-1. (continued)

AbsoluteLayout	This layout inherits the anchoring of AnchorLayout and adds the ability for left-side and top positioning using AbsoluteData's `left` and `top` properties. For example, using this layout, you can specifiy that the widget is located in a specific location with a specific size.
BorderLayout	This is a multipane, application-oriented UI layout style that supports multiple regions, automatic split bars between regions, and built-in expanding and collapsing of regions. For example, using this layout, you can specifiy that widgets are located in the north, south, and center locations with a collapsible/resizable eastern section.
CardLayout	This layout contains multiple widgets, each fit to the container, where only a single widget can be visible at any given time. This layout is useful for wizards or containers that need to show content at progressing stages.
CenterLayout	CenterLayout centers a single widget within its container.
ColumnLayout	This layout creates structural layouts in a multicolumn format where the width of each column can be specified as a percentage or fixed width, but the height is allowed to vary based on the content.
FillLayout	FillLayout places its child components in a horizontal or vertical row, forcing them all to be the same identical size. This layout extends RowLayout.
FitLayout	This layout supports a single widget that automatically expands to fill the layout's container.
FlowLayout	This layout renders each child component into its container using normal browser element flow. This is the default layout for all containers.
FormLayout	A specialized layout that only supports form field widgets. This layout correctly positions and sizes field widgets and adds a text label.
HBoxLayout	A layout that lays its child components in a horizontal row, offering many flexible sizing and positioning options. This layout extends BoxLayout.

Table 4-1. (continued)

RowLayout	This layout positions the container's children in a single horiztontal or vertical row. Each component may specify its height and width in pixels or as a percentage.
TableLayout	This layout allows you to easily render content into an HTML table. The layout, based on a total column count, correctly places widgets into table rows and columns.
TableRowLayout	This is a single-row TableLayout that lays out widgets in multiple columns with a single horizontal row.
VBoxLayout	A layout that lays its child components in a vertical row, offering many flexible sizing and positioning options. This layout extends BoxLayout.

Layout managers utilize *layout data* to provide layout hints when executing the layout. Each layout manager has a specific layout data class that provides hint information for each specific layout.

Most of the layout managers are quite straightforward in their use; you simply use the setLayout method of the container to enable the layout manager for the container. You can then use a specialized add method for adding widgets to the container. The add method also accepts a second parameter, an appropriate LayoutData-derived object, which conveniently allows you to apply layout hints for each child widget you add.

As mentioned earlier, layout managers execute when layout() is called, which in turn delegates to onLayout() and renders all the container's child widgets—onLayout is where all the layout action starts. This method performs the layout and iterates over each child widget, and, using the extracted layout data, applies appropriate layout attributes, creates needed HTML elements, and sets the required sizing and positioning for each widget.

Containers automatically call their layout() method when they are attached to the DOM. In turn, the layout manager's layout() method is called, which means you don't have to call layout() manually unless you add or remove child widgets. This implies that adding child widgets after a layout has executed will result in the widgets not appearing, and this is correct. You need to call layout() if you add a child widget to a container that has rendered.

Note   Always consider how a container will be sized. Some layouts require that the container is correctly sized so that it is able to lay out the container's children. You can size a container either directly, by setting the container's size, or indirectly, through the parent's layout (assuming the container has a parent that sizes its children).

Layout Tips-n-Tricks

Even though using layout managers is not an overly complex task, I've found a few tips that should help you become successful when approaching complex layout problems.

- **Which layout to use**: Every container and any container within another container needs a layout to be defined. Layout mistakes don't generate errors; things just don't render correctly, so it can be hard to figure out what is going wrong. It is best to ensure **all** containers have a layout clearly set. I tend to think it a shame that GXT defaults to FlowLayout for all containers, because this can allow lazy mistakes to creep in.

- **Start simple**: Rather than continuously adding more complexity to a large user interface layout, start with individual containers, get the layout correct for each, and then add them as working parts. This will ensure that layout errors are not bleeding into each other.

- **Nest layouts**: Sometimes the easiest solution to a complex layout problem is to nest layouts together. For example, rather than trying to work out how to force a single container's layout to behave in some complex manner, just add two LayoutContainers. Each container can have a different layout and, when combined vertically or horizontally, will produce the desired result in most cases.

- **Turn borders on**: When using LayoutContainer (the base class for arranging layouts), make sure you initially set setBorder to true so that you can visually see the size and position of the container. This can save you hours of wondering why all your widgets are squashed to the left side when, in fact, the layout container itself is the constraint.

- **Who is sizing whom**: Ensure all containers are either specifically sized by a setSize(int,int) method or sized indirectly through a parent layout manager. When relying on a parent layout manager, pay particular attention to the layout data hints to ensure the child containers are being sized as you intended.

Those are really the best tips I can give you for how to master layouts. From here onward, I'll cover each layout manager individually so you have a sound understanding of the various types and how each can be used.

CenterLayout

As layout managers go, CenterLayout is by far the simplest. Leaving sizing for the child widget, it simply sets the position of the child widget to be the center of its parent container. During execution of the layout, CenterLayout simply calls the El.center(Container element) method to center the child widget within its parent container.

AnchorLayout and AbsoluteLayout

AnchorLayout sizes its children but does not position them. By default, the layout calculates measurements from the container size or, optionally, a virtual anchorSize value. Each child widget can set an anchor specification string, which sets the width and height of the widget relative to its parent container.

Anchor specification is a string that contains two values separated by a space character; for example, "50% 100%". The first value is the width, and the second value corresponds to the height. You can use percentage values or any positive or negative integer values. Integers are treated as offsets from the right and bottom edge, respectively.

AbsoluteLayout extends AnchorLayout and adds positioning support with X and Y locations specified as the left and top of the child widget relative to the parent container.

Listing 4-1 demonstrates AnchorLayout and AbsoluteLayout in action.

Listing 4-1. AnchorLayout and AbsoluteLayout

```
Viewport viewport = new Viewport();
viewport.setLayout(new AnchorLayout());

ContentPanel cp = new ContentPanel();
cp.setHeading("Layout Example");
cp.setLayout(new AbsoluteLayout());

cp.add(new Button("15,20"), new AbsoluteData(15,20));
cp.add(new Button("150,10"), new AbsoluteData(150,10));
cp.add(new Button("25,60"), new AbsoluteData(25,60));

viewport.add(cp, new AnchorData("100% 50%", new Margins(10)));
RootPanel.get().add(viewport);
```

FitLayout and FlowLayout

FlowLayout is the default layout for all containers, so if you fail to set a layout for any container, you'll be using FlowLayout. Using this layout results in normal browser flow, where the elements are rendered starting at the top left and flow downward. Each widget needs to handle its own sizing requirements, as the layout will not size children within the container.

FitLayout supports only a single widget and expands/sizes this single child widget to fit the entire available space in the parent container.

In Figure 4-1, the first panel, titled "Fit," shows a container sized by FitLayout; the second panel, titled "Flow," shows two containers that are self-sized and placed by the layout one after the other.

Figure 4-1. FitLayout and FlowLayout example

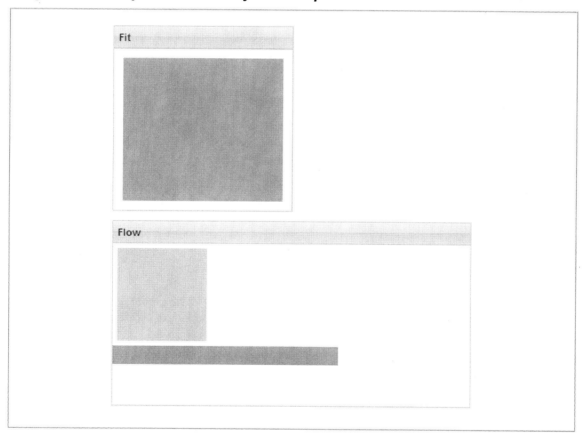

FitLayout and FlowLayout both support setting margins for child widgets using MarginData or their respective subclasses, FitData and FlowData.

Listing 4-2 demonstrates FitLayout and FlowLayout in action.

Listing 4-2. FitLayout and FlowLayout

```
Viewport viewport = new Viewport();

ContentPanel cp = new ContentPanel();
cp.setHeading("Fit");
cp.setLayout(new FitLayout());
Html h = new Html("");
h.setStyleAttribute("backgroundColor", "#FF9999");
cp.add(h,new FitData(10));
cp.setSize(200, 200);
viewport.add(cp ,new MarginData(10));

cp = new ContentPanel();
cp.setHeading("Flow");
cp.setLayout(new FlowLayout());
h = new Html("");
h.setSize(100, 100);
h.setStyleAttribute("backgroundColor", "#99FF99");
cp.add(h,new FlowData(5));
h = new Html("");
h.setSize(250, 20);
h.setStyleAttribute("backgroundColor", "#9999FF");
cp.add(h);
cp.setSize(400, 200);
viewport.add(cp ,new MarginData(0,10,10,10));

RootPanel.get().add(viewport);
```

AccordianLayout and CardLayout

AccordianLayout and CardLayout both extend FitLayout, and thus size their child widgets but do not position them. Both layout managers provide specific functionality for displaying only a single widget at a time.

AccordianLayout is an expandable/collapsible set of ContentPanels that shows only a single active ContentPanel at any time, in an accordion style. All children added to the container must be ContentPanel instances.

CardLayout allows multiple widgets, each sized to fill the container, but only a single widget can be visible at any given time. Any widget can be added to the container. This layout style is most commonly used for wizards and tab implementations where you need to switch quickly back and forth between visible content.

Listing 4-3 demonstrates AccordianLayout and CardLayout in action.

Listing 4-3. AccordianLayout and CardLayout

```
Viewport viewport = new Viewport();
viewport.setLayout(new AccordionLayout());

ContentPanel cp = new ContentPanel();
cp.setHeading("Inbox");
CardLayout cl = new CardLayout();
cp.setLayout(cl);

Html h1 = new Html("Page1");
Html h2 = new Html("Page2");
Html h3 = new Html("Page3");
cl.setActiveItem(h2);
cp.add(h1);
cp.add(h2);
cp.add(h3);

viewport.add(cp);
cp = new ContentPanel();
cp.setHeading("Sent Items");
viewport.add(cp);
cp = new ContentPanel();
cp.setHeading("Drafts");
viewport.add(cp);
RootPanel.get().add(viewport);
```

RowLayout and FillLayout

RowLayout positions its children in a single horizontal or vertical row. Using RowData, each component may specify its height and width in pixels or as a percentage, and may optionally include a margin.

FillLayout extends RowLayout and places its components in a single row or column, forcing them to be of equal size, filling the container. Like RowLayout, margins can be specified by using FillData.

In Figure 4-2, the first panel, titled "Row," shows two containers sized by RowLayout. The first container is sized to fill 100 percent of the available space. The second container has its width sized to 80 percent of the available space, and the container's height is sized to 50 percent. The panel, titled "Fill," shows two containers that are sized to fill the available space, with the second container having a 10-pixel margin.

Figure 4-2. RowLayout and FillLayout example

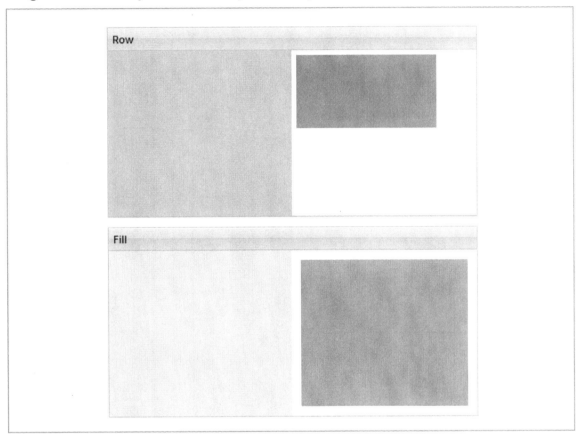

Listing 4-4 demonstrates RowLayout and FillLayout in action.

Listing 4-4. RowLayout and FillLayout

```
Viewport viewport = new Viewport();

ContentPanel cp = new ContentPanel();
cp.setHeading("Row");
cp.setLayout(new RowLayout(Orientation.HORIZONTAL));
Html h = new Html("");
h.setStyleAttribute("backgroundColor", "#99FF99");
```

```
cp.add(h,new RowData(200,200));
h = new Html("");
h.setStyleAttribute("backgroundColor", "#9999FF");
cp.add(h,new RowData(.8,.5 ,new Margins(5)));
cp.setSize(400, 200);
viewport.add(cp , new MarginData(10));

cp = new ContentPanel();
cp.setHeading("Fill");
cp.setLayout(new FillLayout(Orientation.HORIZONTAL));
h = new Html("");
h.setStyleAttribute("backgroundColor", "#FFFF99");
cp.add(h);
h = new Html("");
h.setStyleAttribute("backgroundColor", "#FF99FF");
cp.add(h ,new FillData(10));
cp.setSize(400, 200);
viewport.add(cp , new MarginData(0, 10, 10, 10));

RootPanel.get().add(viewport);
```

HBoxLayout and VBoxLayout

As flexible layout managers, both HBoxLayout and VBoxLayout extend BoxLayout and arrange children in vertical or horizontal rows of boxes according to a set of layout options. To size and position child widgets, these layout managers use one or a combination of the following options:

- **Pack**: Options are Start, Center, or End. Positioning of the widgets relative to the box depends on the layout. For example, Pack-Start places widgets near the top for VBoxLayout and on the left side for HBoxLayout.

- **Align**: Options are Left, Center, Stretch, or StretchMax. Stretch expands (stretches) widgets to the width (or height) of the box. StretchMax stretches widgets to the maximum size of the widest (or tallest) widget in the box.

- **Flex**: An optional layout data hint that tells the layout to use all available space for this widget. Flex also accepts ratio values, so that more space can be allocated to a particular widget.

Note   Some of these options behave relative to the layout in use. For example, Align-Stretch applies to a widget's width for VBoxLayout and a widget's height for HBoxLayout.

ColumnLayout, TableLayout, and TableRowLayout

ColumnLayout is a fairly simple layout manager. It simply adjusts the width of the container's children based on the value of the ColumnData width. If the ColumnData width value is greater than 1.0, the child widget will be set to that width in pixels. If the ColumnData width value is less than 1.0 but greater than 0.0, the child widget will be set to a percentage of the remaining parent container width.

TableLayout is fundamentally a layout manager that uses the HTML Table element as its underlying layout structure. If you are slightly familiar with HTML tables, then you should have a fairly good understanding of the features and capabilities of TableLayout.

TableRowLayout extends TableLayout, with very similar features and layout capabilities, but only offers a single row.

In Figure 4-3, three buttons are laid out within a container set with TableLayout.

Figure 4-3. TableLayout example

Listing 4-5 demonstrates TableLayout.

Listing 4-5. TableLayout

```
Viewport viewport = new Viewport();

LayoutContainer lc = new LayoutContainer();
TableLayout tl = new TableLayout(3);
tl.setBorder(1);
tl.setWidth("100%");
tl.setHeight("200px");
lc.setLayout(tl);
```

```
TableData td = new TableData();
td.setVerticalAlign(VerticalAlignment.TOP);
lc.add(new Button("c1"), td);
td = new TableData();
td.setHorizontalAlign(HorizontalAlignment.CENTER);
lc.add(new Button("c2"), td);
td = new TableData();
td.setHorizontalAlign(HorizontalAlignment.RIGHT);
td.setVerticalAlign(VerticalAlignment.BOTTOM);
lc.add(new Button("c3"), td);
lc.setSize(400, 200);
viewport.add(lc, new MarginData(10));

RootPanel.get().add(viewport);
```

BorderLayout

As a layout manager, BorderLayout is a little more advanced, providing a few extra features in addition to executing a layout. As described in Table 4-1, BorderLayout has center, northern, southern, eastern, and western regions. All outer regions are sizable and collapsible.

To enable the collapsible feature, add a ContentPanel to the region and ensure the BorderLayoutData has setCollapsible set to true. (BorderLayoutData is where you specify things like whether the region is sizeable.) If the region is collapsible, an expand/collapse tool button is automatically rendered in the title bar of the region. If the region is sizeable, BorderLayout renders the borders of that region to automatically have split bars, allowing the user to resize the region within the minimum and maximum sizes you specify.

Another interesting feature of BorderLayout is that it remembers the last collapsed/expanded state and size of each region by using StateManager. This saved data can be cleared by calling panel.clearState() for each region's panel.

A typical use of BorderLayout is shown in Figure 4-4.

Figure 4-4. BorderLayout example

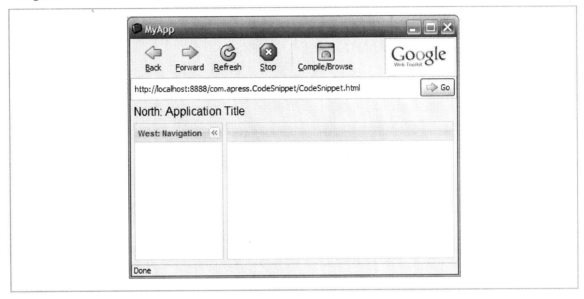

Listing 4-6 shows how the BorderLayout example was constructed.

Listing 4-6. BorderLayout

```
Viewport viewport = new Viewport();
BorderLayout bl = new BorderLayout();
viewport.setLayout(bl);

LayoutContainer north = new LayoutContainer();
north.addText("North: Application Title");
ContentPanel west = new ContentPanel();
west.setHeading("West: Navigation");
ContentPanel center = new ContentPanel();

BorderLayoutData northData
    = new BorderLayoutData(LayoutRegion.NORTH, 20);
northData.setMargins(new Margins(5, 5, 0, 5));

BorderLayoutData westData
    = new BorderLayoutData(LayoutRegion.WEST, 150);
westData.setCollapsible(true);
westData.setFloatable(true);
westData.setSplit(true);
westData.setMargins(new Margins(5, 0, 5, 5));
```

```
BorderLayoutData centerData
= new BorderLayoutData(LayoutRegion.CENTER);
centerData.setMargins(new Margins(5));

viewport.add(north, northData);
viewport.add(west, westData);
viewport.add(center, centerData);

RootPanel.get().add(viewport);
```

FormLayout

FormLayout is a specialized layout manager for dealing with forms. Essentially, the layout builds the form vertically, adds labels, and provides a correct amount of padding and margin for each field.

The next section covers the implementation details of building forms, but here I'll mention one important consideration for using the FormLayout layout manager: FormLayout is designed to work with widgets that are instances of Field.

Caution   As FormLayout will only lay out widgets that extend Field, any widget you add that isn't derived from Field won't be added to the container and won't be rendered. This is an easy mistake to make, as Container allows you to add any widget that extends Component.

AdapterField (which extends Field) provides support for wrapping widget subclasses so you can add any widget to a container using FormLayout.

Forms

Forms are a staple part of a web application diet. You need forms for data input, data display, and user interaction. The GXT package com.extjs.gxt.ui.client.widget.form is dedicated to forms and contains a smorgasbord of widgets.

To assist with the organization and layout of form widgets, GXT provides a container, FormPanel, and layout manager, FormLayout.

FormPanel, a subclass of ContentPanel, is configured with the FormLayout layout manager by default and also provides support for submitting form field data using an HTTP POST or GET request. In addition, it also contains some convenience methods for interacting with field validation.

FormLayout, introduced in the previous section, provides specialized support for adding labels to fields and laying out widgets suitably aligned in a vertical fashion.

Tip   FormPanel may not be suitable for all situations with forms. It can sometimes be more effective to add FormLayout to a dialog or an existing container.

Field, the base class for Form fields, provides default event handling, value handling and validation, and invalid error message indication. All Form widgets extend Field and utilize much of its base implementation.

There are a large number of widgets that extend Field and provide a specific field function. Table 4-2 lists all the Form widgets along with a short description and purpose.

Table 4-2. List of the Available Form Widgets

WIDGET	DESCRIPTION / PURPOSE
AdapterField	Allows any widget to be used in FormLayout by wrapping the widget in a Field subclass.
CheckBox	Single check box (or tick box) field button. Can be used alone or with CheckBoxGroup.
CheckBoxGroup	A group of CheckBox widgets that adds support for aligning all check boxes together horizontally or vertically.
ComboBox	A drop-down combo box field that supports complex data types using ModelData objects.
DateField	A date input field with a DatePicker drop-down and date validation.
FieldSet	A container that draws a border around the form widgets, supports a title, and provides collapsible/expandable functionality.
FileUploadField	A file upload field with an associated browse button.
FormPanel	A ContentPanel for displaying form widgets and submitting them. Includes form submit and validation support.
HiddenField	A field for hidden values that need to be passed in the form submit.

Table 4-2. (continued)

HtmlEditor	A lightweight HTML editor that provides WYSIWYG editing for rich text content.
LabelField	Displays static text for a label.
ListField	A multiselect list field based on ListView that supports complex data types using ModelData objects.
MultiField	A field that displays multiple fields in a single row or column. Superclass of CheckBoxGroup and RadioGroup.
NumberField	A text field that has automatic key filtering and numeric validation.
Radio	Single radio field similar to a check box, but with a round radio button. Can be used alone or with CheckBoxGroup.
RadioGroup	A group of Radio widgets that adds support for aligning all radio buttons together horizontally or vertically. Also ensures only a single radio button in the group can be selected.
SimpleComboBox	A ComboBox subclass that supports any simple data types by internally wrapping provided types into ModelData objects.
TextArea	A text field that supports multiple lines (plain text only).
TextField	Basic text field for raw/plain text input.
TimeField	A field with a time drop-down and automatic time validation.
TriggerField	A TextField that adds a clickable trigger button (like ComboBox).
TwinTriggerField	A two-trigger version of TriggerField.

As you can clearly see, there is a large number of Form widgets that provide numerous options for you to interact with, manage, and display data input.

Rather than provide examples of each widget, I'll demonstrate a simple form with some basic initial features and an advanced form that can submit data and showcases a two-column layout.

A Form Example

Listing 4-7 is the complete code that produces the Personal Information form in Figure 4-5. You can use this example in your own application.

Listing 4-7. Personal Information Form

```java
final FormPanel fp = new FormPanel();
fp.setHeading("Personal Information");
fp.setFrame(true);

TextField fn = new TextField();
fn.setFieldLabel("First name");
fn.setEmptyText("Must not be blank");
fn.setAllowBlank(false);
fp.add(fn);
TextField ln = new TextField();
ln.setFieldLabel("Last name");
fp.add(ln);
TextField em = new TextField();
em.setFieldLabel("Email");
em.setAllowBlank(false);
em.setSelectOnFocus(true);
final String emailReg
  = "[A-Z0-9._%+-]+@[A-Z0-9.-]+\\.[A-Z]{2,4}";
final String errMsg = "Not a valid email address!";
em.setValidator(new Validator<String,
  TextField<String>>() {
      public String validate(TextField<String>
  field, String value) {
          if (!value.toUpperCase().matches(emailReg)) {
            return errMsg;
          }
          return null;
      }
    });
fp.add(em, new FormData("80%"));
TextArea ad = new TextArea();
ad.setFieldLabel("Address");
fp.add(ad, new FormData(270, 100));

Radio radio = new Radio();
radio.setName("radio");
radio.setBoxLabel("Male");
radio.setValue(true);

Radio radio2 = new Radio();
radio2.setName("radio");
radio2.setBoxLabel("Female");

RadioGroup radioGroup = new RadioGroup("test");
```

```
radioGroup.setFieldLabel("Sex");
radioGroup.add(radio);
radioGroup.add(radio2);
fp.add(radioGroup);

SimpleComboBox<String> combo;
combo = new SimpleComboBox<String>();
combo.add("Small");
combo.add("Medium");
combo.add("Large");
combo.add("Xtra Large");
combo.setFieldLabel("Shirt Size");
combo.setEditable(false);
combo.setSimpleValue("Large");
fp.add(combo);

CheckBox check1 = new CheckBox();
check1.setBoxLabel("Brochures");

CheckBox check2 = new CheckBox();
check2.setBoxLabel("Events");
check2.setValue(true);

CheckBox check3 = new CheckBox();
check3.setBoxLabel("Announcements");

CheckBoxGroup checkGroup = new CheckBoxGroup();
checkGroup.setFieldLabel("Subscribe");
checkGroup.add(check1);
checkGroup.add(check2);
checkGroup.add(check3);
fp.add(checkGroup);

Button save = new Button("Save");
save.addSelectionListener(
 new SelectionListener<ComponentEvent>() {
  public void componentSelected(ComponentEvent ce) {
    fp.isValid();
  }
});
fp.getButtonBar().add(save);
fp.getButtonBar().add(new Button("Cancel"));

fp.setWidth(400);
fp.setFieldWidth(270);
fp.setPosition(10, 10);
fp.layout();
```

```
RootPanel.get().add(fp);
```

You'll notice the first field (First name) uses a built-in validation constraint (allowBlank, set to false). This demonstrates the validation and error message features of GXT that make building powerful and fully interactive forms easy.

You can also use custom validators, and I've added one to the Email text field. I used a regular expression string, which will be used to validate the e-mail text. You simply create an implementation of Validator and, in the validate method, return either an error message string if the field is invalid or null if the field is OK.

I've also used SimpleComboBox, which hides a lot of the complexity required by the base ComboBox. Internally, SimpleComboBox wraps the supplied generic type with a SimpleComboValue. This is all handled internally, and generally you'll never need to be aware of it.

Both the Radio and CheckBox fields are grouped so that the label and layout are correct. The grouping also ensures the radio selection is modal, meaning that only one radio button can be selected at any time.

Figure 4-5. Personal Information Form example

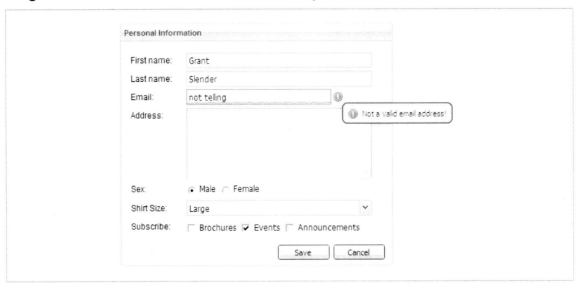

FormLayout, by default, sizes the fields to the default width of 210 pixels; in the example, I've adjusted this to work with the increased width of the container. You can also set the width and height of each field using the FormData layout data hint.

Note   You can't use the widget's `setWidth` and `setHeight` methods when using FormLayout. The layout manager overrides these and sets them during layout. You may remember from the previous section that the layouts are responsible for sizing and positioning.

Form's Rich Text Editor

GXT 2.0 added a rich text editor (or WYSIWIG editor) widget, named HtmlEditor. As its name suggests, the underlying source data is HTML.

To use HtmlEditor, you simply add it like any other Form widget. In Listing 4-8, I've set the label alignment to TOP so that the HtmlEditor can be set to 100 percent width. A submit/cancel button is added to the form, and a listener on the submit button writes the editor's HTML text to the console when the user presses it.

Listing 4-8. HtmlEditor

```
final FormPanel fp = new FormPanel();
fp.setHeading("Comments/Feedback");
fp.setFrame(true);
fp.setLabelAlign(LabelAlign.TOP);
fp.setLabelSeparator("");

final HtmlEditor ed = new HtmlEditor();
ed.setFieldLabel(
"Please Enter Your Comments/Feedback...");
ed.setHeight(200);
fp.add(ed, new FormData("100%"));

fp.setButtonAlign(HorizontalAlignment.RIGHT);
Button submit = new Button("Submit");
fp.addButton(submit);
SelectionListener listener
 = new SelectionListener<ButtonEvent>(){
  public void componentSelected(ButtonEvent ce) {
    System.out.println(ed.getValue());
}
};
submit.addSelectionListener(listener);
fp.addButton(new Button("Cancel"));

fp.setBounds(10, 10, 600, 300);
fp.layout();
RootPanel.get().add(fp);
```

Listing 4-8 produces the form shown in Figure 4-6.

Figure 4-6. HtmlEditor example

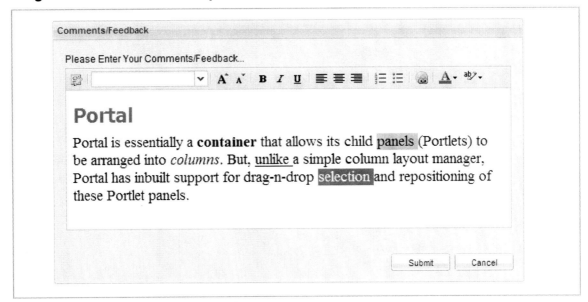

Portal

Portal is essentially a container that allows its child panels (Portlets) to be arranged into columns, as shown in Figure 4-7. Unlike a simple column layout manager, Portal has built-in support for drag-n-drop selection and Portlet repositioning.

Figure 4-7. Portal example

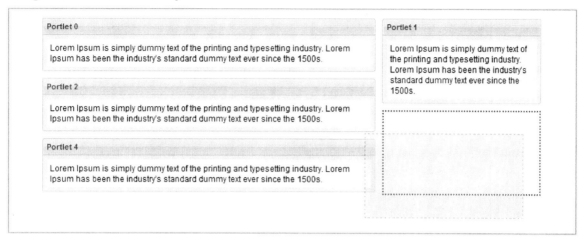

To use Portal, you must first decide how many columns you need and then set the width for each column. Then, add as many Portlets as you need to the Portal container. Portlets are a subclass of ContentPanel and, therefore, offer the same features and styles.

Listing 4-9 creates a Portal and adds five Portlets.

Listing 4-9. Portal

```
Portal p = new Portal(2);
p.setSize("100%", "100%");
p.setColumnWidth(0, .67);
p.setColumnWidth(1, .33);

for (int n=0;n<5;n++) {
   Portlet pl = new Portlet();
   pl.setHeading("Portlet "+n);

   pl.addText(CodeSnippet.getBogusText());
   p.add(pl, n%2);
}
RootPanel.get().add(p);
```

Drag-n-Drop

Drag-n-Drop (DnD) is part of the com.extjs.gxt.ui.client.dnd package. This package contains two base classes, DragSource and DragTarget, which provide the fundamental mechanics for how DnD is handled within GXT.

From these base classes, you can implement your own DnD functionality to any widget. If you only wish to add DnD to Grid, Tree, or ListView, the following three DragSource and DragTarget subclasses are provided:

- **GridDragSource and GridDragTarget**: Aimed at the Grid widget, these provide single and multiple row selections for source, and allow insert and appends as targets for rows.

- **TreeDragSource and TreeDragTarget**: Aimed at the Tree widget, these provide single tree item selection for source, and allow appends into tree parent nodes as well as re-ordering by targeting itself.

- **ListViewDragSource and ListViewDragTarget**: Aimed at the ListView widget, these provide the same features as GridDragSource and GridDragTarget.

In Listing 4-10, I created two lists and populated one list with a store containing a bunch of CarModels. CodeSnippet.getCars() just returns a List<CarModel>. Essentially, the ListViews do not have to be the same, but they do need to have the same model so that an item dragged from a source is suitable for dropping onto the target. In saying that, I've changed the display template for both lists so you can see that GXT actually handles the data internally and appends the CarModel into the other list.

The setup for DnD is really straightforward. You define the DragSource and DragTarget for each type of widget. In this example, we want to be able to drag and drop from and to both lists, so we configure source and target for both the left and right list.

Listing 4-10. DnD

```
ContentPanel cp = new ContentPanel();
cp.setHeading("ListView Drag-n-Drop");
cp.setSize(400, 175);
cp.setFrame(true);
cp.setLayout(new RowLayout(Orientation.HORIZONTAL));

ListView<CarModel> leftList = new ListView<CarModel>();
leftList.setSimpleTemplate("<b>{car_make}</b>
 {car_model} <i>({car_year})</i>");
leftList.setDisplayProperty("name");
ListStore<CarModel> store = new ListStore<CarModel>();
store.add(CodeSnippet.getCars());
leftList.setStore(store);

ListView<CarModel> rightList = new ListView<CarModel>();
rightList.setSimpleTemplate("{car_year}
 {car_make} {car_model}");
store = new ListStore<CarModel>();
rightList.setStore(store);
```

```
RowData data = new RowData(.5, 1);
data.setMargins(new Margins(5));
cp.add(leftList, data);
cp.add(rightList, data);

new ListViewDragSource(leftList);
new ListViewDropTarget(leftList);

new ListViewDragSource(rightList);
new ListViewDropTarget(rightList);

RootPanel.get().add(cp);
```

XTemplates

XTemplate is a class that supports advanced functionality for dealing with HTML fragments. Using XTemplates you can auto-fill data using arrays, and include conditional processing with basic support for comparison operators, subtemplates, math functions, and variables. XTemplates can also be compiled so that the fragment is evaluated and a reference saved, ensuring the fragment can be rendered very quickly whenever needed.

Starting life as an Ext JS feature, XTemplates have been included in GXT so that similar templating techniques developed in Ext JS can be used in GXT. Documentation on XTemplates can be found on the Ext JS web site (http://extjs.com/docs).

Chapter 3 outlined an introduction to XTemplates as part of the ListView example. In Listing 4-11, a simple template was used to map property names into an HTML fragment. That template was internally used by ListView as the inline display for the list.

Listing 4-11 shows a more concrete example of how templates are used to iterate over the elements within an array to render HTML directly into a widget's Element object.

The first two lines build the HTML fragment using the tpl tag and the for operator. If the variable in the for operator is an array, it will iterate over the text between the tags.

The next lines create an XTemplate instance and an array of names. Those names are converted to a JavaScriptObject, which is required by XTemplate (as internally it's optimized Ext JavaScript code).

Finally, the Html widget is created, and its onRender method overridden, whereby the XTemplate is told to overwrite the Element with the fragment using the JavaScript array object.

Listing 4-11. XTemplate

```
String text = "Customer Name: {.}<br>";
String html = "<tpl for=\".\">"+text+"</tpl>";

final XTemplate t = XTemplate.create(html);
String[] names = { "Tom", "Mary", "Bob", "Jill" };

final JavaScriptObject jsArray
 = JsUtil.toJavaScriptArray(names);

Html h = new Html() {
   protected void onRender(Element target, int index) {
      super.onRender(target, index);
      t.overwrite(target, jsArray);
   }
};
RootPanel.get().add(h);
```

Summary

Whew! We've covered a few advanced things in this chapter. Having a solid understanding of how layouts work is important, as they are fundamental to how you construct and organize widgets within GXT. Hopefully the lengthy section on layouts has given you the confidence to build some *advanced,* rich Internet applications. The coverage on Forms, Portal, and Drag-n-Drop rounded out the chapter on advanced stuff.

In the next chapter, I'll continue the advanced theme, but focus totally on APIs that work with large amounts of data—Data, Stores, and Loaders—and the widget that displays things, Grid. This framework helps manage data to and from the server, provides local caching, and provides a unique way to have introspection in GWT and yet still use POJOs on the server side.

Chapter 5: Working With Data

When you build a rich Internet application, you are not just dealing with widgets and visual layouts: you also need to display and represent data to the user in a manner that is both visually agile and dynamic, but also structured and measured. This challenge requires efficient management of local data so that you can quickly and effectively redisplay data shown previously, but in different ways, such as through sorting, filtering, and grouping, to name a few.

This chapter covers how GXT provides this flexibility and advanced management of local data in ways that will truly make your application shine. Using data objects like ModelData and BeanModel, and local caching systems like stores and loaders, you will be able to take advantage of the most advanced data widgets—Grid, Table, Tree, and ListView.

Data, Stores, and Loaders

By now you've probably seen the mention of data models and stores. In this section, I'm going to provide a good understanding of how they work. You'll need that understanding as we proceed through the rest of the chapter.

Models

GXT uses ModelData as its data type. ModelData objects can be thought of as your *User Interface* model (or local domain object), with added support for data introspection. So while GWT doesn't support Java reflection, ModelData provides a degree of introspection that allows the widget to inspect property names and values. This allows a widget to interrogate data objects without having to have concrete support for any particular data type, providing separation from the model and view.

BaseModel is the base class that you extend to create your own data model within GXT. Listing 5-1 shows an example data model (CarModel) that you'll use in the Grid examples later in this chapter.

Listing 5-1. CarModel

```java
public class CarModel extends BaseModel {

  public CarModel(String mk, String ml, Integer y) {
    set("car_make", mk);
    set("car_model", ml);
    set("car_year", y);
  }

  public CarModel(String mk, String ml,
  Integer y, Double v) {
    this(mk, ml, y);
    set("car_value", v);
  }

  public String getMake() {
    return (String)get("car_make");
  }

  public Integer getYear() {
    return (Integer)get("car_year");
  }
}
```

You'll notice that there are no local fields within the model. All local data is stored within the BaseModel's set/get methods, which internally store all data within a HashMap.

Stores

GXT has a concept of a store, which contains a local copy of the data (or model data) that you wish to display or manipulate. Some data widgets can work directly with this store (like ListView, Grid, and ComboBox), and some data widgets require an intermediate binding function to build child data widgets from the store contents (like Table, Tree, and DataList).

Store and its subclasses implement a local cache of the data objects that you would use in your application. A local cache of the data is maintained so that you can sort, filter, and modify the data locally. The store uses the event system to notify widgets that new data has arrived or that a sort has been applied. Widgets that work directly with the store add and remove data objects as needed, and obtain Record objects to track modifications to data.

Caution　　You need to be realistic about the size of what you can store locally. For example, manipulating 100,000 records ain't going to perform very well within the browser. As such, consider this early in your application design and ensure that only a sensible amount of data is transferred to the client.

Loaders

Two options exist for getting data into the store. You can manually add data objects directly or use the GXT Loader. Loaders provide convenient methods for dealing with data obtained via Remote Procedure Call (RPC), XML, or JSON and converting remote data into ModelData instances. Loader performs this task by using a proxy to remotely fetch data, and the conversion is enabled by a reader.

This all sounds fairly complex, and it is, so to help illustrate the relationships, I've provided a diagram in Figure 5-1 that outlines how remote XML data is obtained and manipulated into something used by a Grid widget.

Figure 5-1. How remote XML data gets into the Grid widget

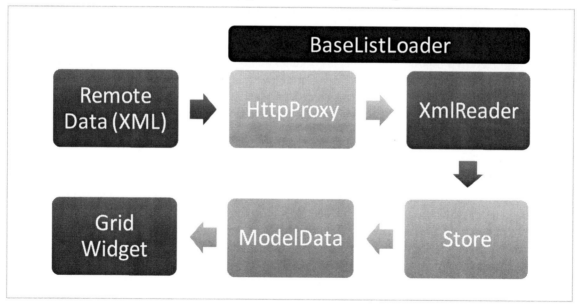

The process for JSON or RPC is the same as illustrated in Figure 5-1 for XML, with the only exception being that RPC does not require a reader—the data objects are already assumed to be ModelData instances.

This last point raises an interesting question: does this mean if I choose to use RPC, I also use GXT ModelData objects at my server and transfer them into and out of my domain objects?

The simple answer is, not unless you want to. You can avoid having GXT among server-side code by using the GXT BeanModel. BeanModel leverages a GWT feature called *deferred binding* to eliminate the need for your domain objects (or JavaBeans) to be instances of ModelData.

GWT DEFERRED BINDING—WHAT THE?

Deferred binding is similar to compile-time Java reflection. JavaScript doesn't support any kind of runtime introspection, so the GWT team added deferred binding support to the GWT compiler.

For example, GWT uses this feature for internationalization to ensure only the English-language Strings are included when the compiler generates permutations for an English-speaking locale. The String text for French, German, etc. are not included in the English permutation or the resulting compiled output, but will be when their respective locales are compiled.

More about deferred binding can be read online in the GWT Developer's Guide at http://tinyurl.com/cato89.

Using GWT deferred bindings, a new class is generated that extends BeanModel. This generated class contains getter/setter implementations for all the field properties of your JavaBean, essentially creating a new ModelData class based on your domain object. In the client application, BeanModelReader is used to convert the domain objects into these "deferred binding"–generated BeanModel objects.

Using BeanModel Objects

There are two ways to identify to GXT that you wish to use BeanModel objects. The first method requires your JavaBean to implement the BeanModelTag interface. Obviously this method requires that you modify your existing domain object. A second method does not require any modification, though it does require creation of a new interface that extends BeanModelMarker and uses annotations to tie the class to your JavaBean.

To understand this better, let me introduce you to the domain object, Customer, as shown in Listing 5-2.

Listing 5-2. The Customer Class

```
public class Customer {
  private String firstname;
  private String lastname;

  public Customer() {
  }

  public Customer (String firstname, String lastname) {
    setFirstname(firstname);
    setLastname(lastname);
  }

  public String getFirstname() {
    return firstname;
  }

  public void setFirstname(String firstname) {
    this.firstname = firstname;
  }

  public String getLastname() {
    return lastname;
  }
}
```

Now you need to create a new class that identifies to GXT that you want to generate BeanModels. To do this, create a new interface class, add an @BEAN annotation, and ensure that it extends BeanModelMarker. Listing 5-3 provides an example based on the recently created Customer class .

Listing 5-3. The CustomerBeanModel Interface

```
@BEAN(com.apress.data.Customer.class)
public interface CustomerBeanModel extends BeanModelMarker {
}
```

Once you've marked your bean as shown Listing 5-3, you've done what's needed to start using BeanModels. To create a BeanModel instance based on your domain object (perhaps to create a new customer), you need to use BeanModelFactory to create a model instance. This is accomplished by using BeanModelLookup to get an instance of BeanModelFactory, as shown in Listing 5-4.

Listing 5-4. Creating a CustomerBeanModel

```
BeanModelFactory factory = BeanModelLookup.get().getFactory(Customer.class);
Customer c = new Customer("Tim","Smith");
BeanModel model = factory.createModel(c);
```

You'll be using Customer and CustomerBeanModel in the example application in Chapter 6.

Stores and Loaders

Stores provide local caching of ModelData objects and also support filtering and sorting of those cached objects. There are two types of stores within GXT: a ListStore designed for lists of data (like tables, grids, and views), and a TreeStore designed for hierarchical data. As you can guess, TreeStore is used when the Tree widget is used.

When editing models, the store provides a Record object so that changes to a model can be tracked. The before and after changes are captured for each model so that you can commit all changes, or if needed, roll one or all of them back. Using the getRecord(M model) method in Store, you can obtain the current instance of the Record object. Using the commitChanges() or rejectChanges() methods, you can tell Store to update or discard the outstanding changes.

Stores use events to communicate changes to store contents. A store listener contains the following events:

- Add: Data has been added to the store.

- Clear: The store has been cleared of data.

- BeforeDataChanged: This is fired before data changes (e.g., before loading).

- DataChanged: Data has changed (e.g., just loaded).

- Filter: A filter has been applied.

- Remove: Data has been removed.

- Sort: The store has been sorted.

- Update: Data has been updated via its Record.

As previously mentioned, you can load data into ListStore manually using the add(M model) or add(List<M> models) methods. Getting the data to the client, converting or transferring it into a ModelData subclass, is also a task that you'll have to perform.

Alternatively, you can use a loader, which is designed to assist in the correct loading and converting of data into a store. Similar to stores, BaseListLoader is for lists, and BaseTreeLoader is for hierarchies. There is also a third type of loader, a paging loader that, as its name implies, is designed to assist loaders that can page data into the store. This is useful for situations where you just have too much data to provide to the client in a single load. BasePagingLoader provides an offset and limit against the total data available and produces the necessary requests to the server to load this data.

Let's go through an example. Extending the Customer and BeanModel examples, you'll now set up a proxy, loader, and reader to configure the ListStore.

Note   Previously I mentioned that RPC doesn't need a reader, and it doesn't, but obviously if you are converting from JavaBean domain objects into BeanModel objects you'll need something that can convert from one object type into the other, and that is what the BeanModelReader does.

Listing 5-5. Creating and Configuring the ListStore

```
RpcProxy proxy = new RpcProxy() {
  public void load(Object loadCfg, AsyncCallback cb) {
    service.getCustomers(callback);
  }
};

BeanModelReader reader = new BeanModelReader();

ListLoader loader = new BaseListLoader(proxy, reader);
Store store = new ListStore<BeanModel>(loader);
```

Listing 5-5 starts by configuring an RpcProxy and overriding the load(Object,AsyncCallback) method where you call the GWT RPC service getCustomers. Next, you create the BeanModelReader, which internally uses the BeanModel factory to create beans from the returned domain objects. Finally, bind the proxy and reader together with a ListLoader and assign this loader to the ListStore.

If you are new to GWT development, you'll probably find the service.getCustomers(callback) call a little confusing, so let me explain a little more about GWT RPC services.

GWT RPC

When using RPC, GWT needs to create a system of callbacks so that the returning call from the server-side Java bytecode is matched to the compiled GWT JavaScript client-side code.

Like its namesake, RPC is a mechanism for calling methods remotely as if the function or procedure was local. In GWT, the client calls a method against a service definition that returns the requesting data via a system of callbacks.

Google provides a detailed explanation of how GWT RPC works in the online GWT Developer's Guide (http://tinyurl.com/ajecdo). Figure 5-2 contains a copy of Google's GWT RPC plumbing diagram, which outlines the classes that need to be created, their relationship to other RPC classes, and where these objects are executed (client or server).

Figure 5-2. GWT RPC plumbing diagram

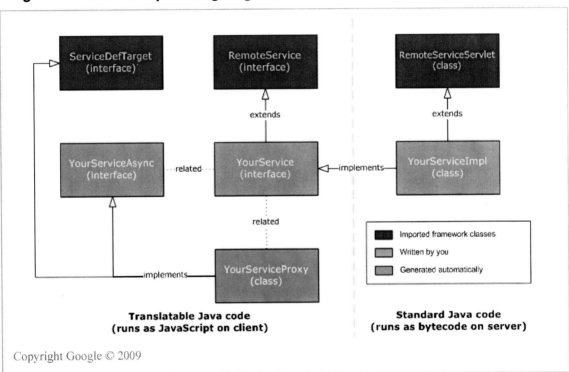

Let's continue the Customer example and step through the setup tasks to start using GWT RPC for both the client and server parts of the application. Start by defining a service interface that includes the method you want the client to call and the server to implement, as shown in Listing 5-6.

Listing 5-6. The MyService Interface

```
public interface MyService extends RemoteService {
    public List<Customer> getCustomers();
}
```

Note that you define the method exactly how you'd like to be able to use it, returning a list of Customer objects. Next, define another similar interface with the same methods, but this time with no return types. You define the parameters of the methods to have an additional item of the type AsyncCallback, which has a type signature of the return type you defined in the previous interface (in this case, it's List<Customer>). Listing 5-7 shows how to do it.

Listing 5-7. The MyServiceAsync Interface

```
public interface MyServiceAsync {
    public void getCustomers(AsyncCallback<List<Customer>> callback);
}
```

Now you're ready to implement the MyService interface for the server. In this step, you create the class in a separate package for the client code, because you don't want the GWT compiler to try and compile this code. It would most likely not compile correctly anyway (mainly because you'd be using a database or Java API not available in GWT). Here you'll use the com.apress.server package, which is the recommended package naming style for GWT server code, but you can use anything as long as it's not the com.apress.client package.

Other than extending RemoteServiceServlet and implementing the MyService interface, there is nothing special about the implementation code. You return the results normally, and you don't have to do anything particularly unique with the objects before passing them on to the client. GWT will take care of the needed transformation and serialization of objects. Listing 5-8 shows the implementation used in the example.

Listing 5-8. The MyServiceImpl Class

```
public class MyServiceImpl extends RemoteServiceServlet implements MyService {

    private Map<String, Customer> customers;

    public List<Customer> getCustomers() {
        if (customers == null) {
            loadCustomers();
        }
        return new ArrayList<Customer>(customers.values());
    }
}
```

Now that you've defined and implemented the server side of things, you need to create a service object within the client application that communicates with the service running on the server.

GWT provides a set of classes for this, and essentially you only have to plumb things together. Listing 5-9 outlines the basic steps needed to get the RPC service working in a client application.

Listing 5-9. Creating an RPC Service

```
MyServiceAsync service;
String moduleURL = GWT.getModuleBaseURL() + "myService"; service =
(MyServiceAsync) GWT.create(MyService.class);
ServiceDefTarget endpoint = (ServiceDefTarget) service;
endpoint.setServiceEntryPoint(moduleURL);
```

The first line defines the service object. GWT will generate this with deferred binding using the MyServiceAsync interface for its definition. In the next line, you create a String that is essentially the URL that the server will be offering the service on. After this, you ask GWT to create a MyService object, knowing it will actually be generated on the MyServiceAsync interface. The last line tells GWT to initialize the service using the URL defined previously.

The final part of this GWT RPC puzzle is to launch the implementation of RemoteServiceServlet when the embedded web server starts. This allows you to continue working within the hosted mode shell and test the service implementation along with the client code. This has recently changed in GWT 1.6 from previous GWT releases. You now create a standard web.xml file, which simplifies the learning for those who are already familiar with J2EE container configuration. Located in the /war/WEB-INF folder, this file will look like Listing 5-10.

Listing 5-10. Updated web.xml File

```
<?xml version="1.0" encoding="UTF-8"?>
<web-app>
  <servlet>
    <servlet-name>myService</servlet-name>
    <servlet-class>com.apress.server.MyServiceImpl</servlet-class>
  </servlet>
  <servlet-mapping>
    <servlet-name>myService</servlet-name>
    <url-pattern>/myapp/myService</url-pattern>
  </servlet-mapping>
</web-app>
```

I won't fully explain the contents of a web.xml file, as this would be well beyond the scope of the book. Suffice to say that the url-pattern needs to match the URL in

`ServiceDefTarget.setServiceEntryPoint`, and the `servlet-class` name needs to match the fully qualified class name of the service implementation.

We've focused a fair bit on enabling the server and client to be able to communicate and share data; now that this is done, you can continue with some widgets that take advantage of all this data. Let's jump into it.

Grid

Grid is a powerful data widget for displaying and editing large lists of related data. Although similar to the Table widget, Grid provides fast and flexible rendering of data and includes built-in support for plug-ins, grouping, summary views, full in-place editing, custom column models, and header menus (supporting hiding, sorting, and grouping). An example of Grid being used to automatically group related data, configurable by the user, is shown in Figure 5-3.

Figure 5-3. A grouping Grid example

Grid uses `ModelData` to define which columns display which properties, and relies on the store to provide a list of `ModelData` objects. As such, you can either add `BaseModelData` objects to the store, or use `BeanModel` to load your domain objects and display them within a grid.

Let's start out with an example the can explain the basic configuration steps when using Grid.

A Basic Grid

While this is a fairly basic example of Grid, it is a bit long, so I'll break it up into parts. The code in Listing 5-11 sets up the parent container and the store.

Listing 5-11. Basic Grid: Set Up Parent and Store

```
LayoutContainer container = new LayoutContainer();
container.setLayout(new FitLayout());

ListStore<CarModel> store = new ListStore<CarModel>();
store.add(CodeSnippet.getCars());
store.sort("car_year", SortDir.ASC);
```

The first lines create a parent container and set the layout to FitLayout. This will ensure Grid fills the entire available space. If the parent's available space is not big enough for either the columns or rows, Grid will automatically add scroll bars and allow scrolling to occur. You don't have to do anything to enable this, other than set a size for the container.

The store is created using CarModel as its type, and data is added to the store by passing it a list of CarModel objects. This is what the call to CodeSnippet.getCars() does. Lastly, sort the store on the car_year field property in ascending order.

You now have to define the columns, and Listing 5-12 shows you how.

Listing 5-12. Basic Grid: Set Up Columns

```
List<ColumnConfig> col = new ArrayList<ColumnConfig>();

ColumnConfig column = new ColumnConfig();
column.setId("car_make");
column.setHeader("Make");
column.setWidth(150);
col.add(column);

column = new ColumnConfig();
column.setId("car_model");
column.setHeader("Model");
column.setWidth(120);
col.add(column);

column = new ColumnConfig();
column.setId("car_year");
column.setHeader("Year");
column.setWidth(80);
```

```
column.setAlignment(HorizontalAlignment.RIGHT);
col.add(column);

ColumnModel cm = new ColumnModel(col);
```

First you create an empty array to hold the ColumnConfigs, and then you create three ColumnConfig objects, using setId to set each column to match the property name set within the CarModel. You should also provide a header title name and an initial column width. When finished, the last line adds the array of ColumnConfigs to a ColumnModel, which holds the configuration for all columns within a Grid.

The final part, shown in Listing 5-13, is to configure the Grid and attach it to RootPanel.

Listing 5-13. Basic Grid: Set Up Grid and Attach

```
Grid grid = new Grid<CarModel>(store, cm);
grid.setBorders(true);
grid.setStripeRows(true);
grid.getView().setForceFit(true);
GridSelectionModel gsm = grid.getSelectionModel();
gsm.setSelectionMode(SelectionMode.SINGLE);
container.add(grid);

container.setSize(300, 200);
container.setPosition(50,50);
RootPanel.get().add(container);
```

The Grid widget itself is created, defined with the CarModel type, and passed the store and ColumnModel. As you're using a parent container with no border or frame, you've enabled the border on the Grid. Striped rows are enabled, and you tell the Grid's view that you wish it to force the columns to expand or contract to avoid showing a horizontal scroll bar. You get a reference to the Grid's selection model, and set the selection mode to only select single rows.

Finally, you add the Grid to the parent container, and then size and position the container and add it to RootPanel. Those three steps are what's basically required to configure a Grid: set up the store, set up the columns, and then set up the Grid itself.

EditorGrid

A Grid that can edit its data isn't significantly more complex. The three steps remain the same, with an additional consideration around the column configuration. As shown in Figure 5-4, the EditorGrid overlays a widget that extends Field when editing is required.

Figure 5-4. First EditorGrid example

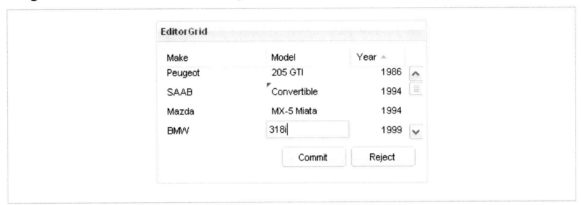

To reproduce the example in Figure 5-4, you need to adjust the container, which will now be a ContentPanel. You'll also allow the container to resize with the browser window, which demonstrates that Grid can resize correctly and automatically show scroll bars as needed. Listing 5-14 provides the code.

Listing 5-14. EditorGrid: Changed Layout and Container

```
Viewport vp = new Viewport();
vp.setLayout(new AbsoluteLayout());
ContentPanel container = new ContentPanel();
container.setFrame(true);
container.setHeading("EditorGrid");
container.setLayout(new FitLayout());
AbsoluteData ad = new AbsoluteData(40,40);
ad.setAnchorSpec("40% 40%");
vp.add(container, ad);
```

The code in Listing 5-14 is not really anything specific to EditorGrid, but I wanted to show you another way to use Grid in a container whereby the container itself is the size constraint, and Grid itself will decide when to show scroll bars.

In Listing 5-15, you add a listener to the standard store so that you can see when the underlying data has changed. From this you can be notified when things have been modified, sorted, or added/removed.

Listing 5-15. EditorGrid: Add Store Listener

```
store.addStoreListener(new StoreListener() {
  public void handleEvent(StoreEvent se) {
    if (se.getType()== Store.DataChanged) {
      System.out.println("DataChanged");
    }
  }
});
...
```

Listing 5-16 shows what the EditorGrid configuration is mostly about. Start by creating a TextField object (if needed, you can also set up validation, etc.) and then use it to create a CellEditor. You do the same thing for NumberField, and create a specific CellEditor for editing number data.

The final step is to assign setEditor on the columns you wish to make editable.

Listing 5-16. EditorGrid: Add Cell Editors

```
TextField tf = new TextField<String>();
CellEditor tce = new CellEditor(tf);
NumberField nf = new NumberField();
nf.setPropertyEditorType(Integer.class);
CellEditor nce = new CellEditor(nf);
...
column.setId("car_make");
column.setEditor(tce);
...
column.setId("car_year");
column.setEditor(nce);
...
```

As far as the Grid itself is concerned, you just change to an EditorGrid, and the rest is fairly similar. I've added some buttons to showcase how you would commit or reject changes within the store, which occurs after editing a cell. Listing 5-17 shows the EditorGrid change and the new buttons added to the container.

Listing 5-17. *EditorGrid: Change from Grid, Add Buttons*

```
EditorGrid grid = new EditorGrid<CarModel>(store, cm);
...
Button b1 = new Button("Commit");
b1.addSelectionListener(new SelectionListener<ButtonEvent>() {
  public void componentSelected(ButtonEvent be) {
    store.commitChanges();
  }
});
Button b2 = new Button("Reject");
b2.addSelectionListener(new SelectionListener<ButtonEvent>() {
  public void componentSelected(ButtonEvent be) {
    store.rejectChanges();
  }
});

container.setButtonAlign(HorizontalAlignment.RIGHT);
container.addButton(b1);
container.addButton(b2);

RootPanel.get().add(vp);
```

This is essentially all that is required for enabling cell-editing support to a Grid, so it seems fairly straightforward, hey?

Unfortunately, it can get a little more complex. In situations where either your model or the Field you'd like to use doesn't natively translate between data types, you'll need to be able to preprocess and postprocess the data objects before and after editing.

Fortunately, GXT again comes to the rescue, and I've prepared another EditorGrid example that showcases how this is easily done. In Figure 5-5, you'll notice we're now using a ComoBox to edit data within a Grid.

Figure 5-5. Second EditorGrid example

To illustrate both model and editor field mismatches, I've created a simple Java enumerated type to be used in the ModelData object.

Note   I love using Enum within Java instead of constant strings or static/final integer values. I think the code it produces is far more readable and ensures that typed values aren't accidentally used incorrectly. In GWT 1.5 and onwards, you have full support for the enum keyword. You can also substitute the use of enumerated types in GXT if you are careful (and a little clever). The main trick is to ensure your enum has a toString() method that allows simple value presentation. As Enum within Java is essentially a class, you can add any type of method to make things easier.

What follows is the FreqType enumerated type. The code in Listing 5-18 is fairly self-explanatory, so I won't detail an explanation.

Listing 5-18. The FreqType Enumerated Type

```
public enum FreqType {
  DAILY("Daily"), WEEKLY("Weekly"),
  FORTNIGHTLY("Fortnightly"), MONTHLY("Monthly"),
  QUARTERLY("Quarterly"), YEARLY("Yearly");

  private String name;

  FreqType(String name) {
    this.name = name;
  }

  public String toString() {
    return name;
  }
}
```

The nice aspect of using Enum with GXT is the simple setup of combo boxes when using SimpleComboBox. In Listing 5-19, you can see how I've been able to set the type as FreqType and then use the Arrays.asList utility method to populate the combo box.

Listing 5-19. SimpleComboBox Using Enum

```
freqCombo = new SimpleComboBox<FreqType>();
freqCombo.setEditable(false);
freqCombo.add(Arrays.asList(FreqType.values()));
```

Now that you've got the data type and editable field organized, let's look at applying this to the EditorGrid. As mentioned before, you can't just add the SimpleComboBox to CellEditor like you did with TextField. If you do, you'll get a ClassCastException every time you try to edit the field. So what goes wrong?

CellEditor will call setValue on the field, and the implementation of setValue in SimpleComboBox expects a ModelData. The value set is obtained from the model, which is a FreqType instance, so BANG! ClassCastException is thrown.

The solution is to override CellEditor's preProcessValue method and convert the object into a type that SimpleComboBox can accept. In Listing 5-20, you'll see I check that the object is an instance of FreqType, and if it is, I ask the combo box to find me the internal model and return that instead.

Listing 5-20. EditorGrid: SimpleComboBox and Custom CellEditor

```
ColumnConfig freq = new ColumnConfig();
freq.setId("freq");
freq.setHeader("Frequency");
freq.setWidth(60);

final SimpleComboBox<FreqType> freqCombo = new SimpleComboBox<FreqType>();
freqCombo.setEditable(false);
freqCombo.add(Arrays.asList(FreqType.values()));
CellEditor freqEditor = new CellEditor(freqCombo) {
  public Object preProcessValue(Object v) {
    if (v instanceof FreqType) {
      return freqCombo.findModel((FreqType)v);
    }
    return FreqType.DAILY;
  }

  public Object postProcessValue(Object value) {
    return ((SimpleComboValue) value).get("value");
  }
};
freq.setEditor(freqEditor);
```

On the flip side, when you finish editing, it's time to convert that SimpleComboValue back into a FreqType model. That's simply done by calling get("value"). The property "value" is defined internally to SimpleComboValue to represent the wrapped type value.

This approach can be applied to any model or editable field problem you encounter when you're not using simple text or number values in your Grid.

Even More Grid

As a final piece on Grid, let's build the grouping and summary part of the example grid shown in Figure 5-3. This code will produce very specific summarized data similar to the rightmost column shown in Figure 5-6. The Grid's rendering code will be configured to group similar data and provide a summary row, adding up the columns during the rendering process.

Figure 5-6. Summarizing data

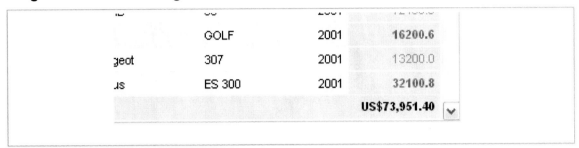

Tip   Using the grouping and summary features of Grid is a really good design idea. As all of this data manipulation is handled internally by the local Grid widget, users get a good degree of flexibility on how the data is presented without having to round-trip back to the server to reprocess the data they already have. Your users will love you for using this Grid feature!

GXT includes two types of grouping views: GroupingView and GroupSummaryView. They both group related data using a defined grouping field, but GroupSummaryView adds the ability to provide a summary row under each set of grouped rows.

To perform the grouping, you need to change to a GroupingStore, which allows you to define a grouped field and internally supports what's needed for the views to show grouped data. Listing 5-21 shows how to set up the store and assign the field to group on.

Listing 5-21. GroupingStore

```
GroupingStore<CarModel> store = new GroupingStore<CarModel>();
store.add(CodeSnippet.getCars());
store.sort("car_year", SortDir.ASC);
store.groupBy("car_year");
...
```

Next, as you also want to summarize the grouped columns into a summary row, you need to convert every ColummConfig into a subclass that supports summary configurations—SummaryColumnConfig.

By default, none of the columns will actually summarize anything unless you set a SummaryType, which in this example will be SummaryType.SUM for the "car_value" column.

SummaryType includes three default actions: SUM, which adds the values together; AVG, which provides an average; and COUNT, which counts the rows. As you are summarizing $ value information, you also set the summary format to a currency NumberFormat.

Listing 5-22. SummaryColumnConfig

```
column = new SummaryColumnConfig();
NumberFormat nf = NumberFormat.getCurrencyFormat();
column.setSummaryFormat(nf);
column.setSummaryType(SummaryType.SUM);
column.setId("car_value");
column.setHeader("$ Value");
column.setWidth(120);
column.setAlignment(HorizontalAlignment.RIGHT);

column.setRenderer(new GridCellRenderer() {
  public String render(ModelData m, String p,
  ColumnData cd, int r, int c, ListStore s) {
    double v = m.get(p);
    String style = "lighttext";
    if (v>15000) style = "redtext";
    return "<div class="+style+">"+v+"</div>";
  }
});
col.add(column);
...
```

Also in Listing 5-22, you'll notice I set a custom GridCellRenderer. I did this because I wanted the values to be formatted differently depending on the value of the car. The line double v = m.get(p) essentially gets the value from the property (p) using the model (m) and, using Java auto-boxing, converts it to a primitive type (v).

The lines after this simply determine the value. If the value is larger than some arbitrary value ($15,000), the style changes. All rather simple, yet highly effective in how it displays data to the user.

The styles are defined in CSS as shown in Listing 5-23.

Listing 5-23. CSS Styles Used for GridCellRenderer

```
.lighttext {
  color: #888888;
}

.redtext {
  color: #ff0000;
  font-weight: bold;
}
```

The final step in enabling a grouped Grid is to create an instance of GroupSummaryView. You then configure another custom renderer, this time GridGroupRenderer, which is a header row added above the grouped set. In Listing 5-24, you assemble a string of elements that you want to display in the group header.

Listing 5-24. GroupSummaryView

```
GroupSummaryView view = new GroupSummaryView();
view.setForceFit(true);
view.setGroupRenderer(new GridGroupRenderer() {
  public String render(GroupColumnData data) {
    int size = data.models.size();
    String h = cm.getColumnById(data.field).getHeader();
    String itms = size == 1 ? "Item" : "Items";
    itms =  " (" + size + " " + itms + ")";
    return h + ": " + data.group + itms;
  }
});
...
grid.setView(view);
```

The last task is to set the Grid's view to the GroupSummaryView object. All other aspects of the grouping and summary Grid configuration are essentially the same as the basic Grid example.

If you construct the example as I've shown, it won't have the yellow striped rows and the orange summary rows and column shown in Figure 5-3 unless your application has some additional style information.

This style is achieved using custom CSS to override some of the existing GXT styles. The styles in Listing 5-25 are added by the application's local CSS, in this particular case CodeSnippet.css.

As you also want to apply a style to a dynamically generated column (the column assigned the ID of "car_value"), you have to simulate that generated style, labeled x-grid3-td-car_value, in your CSS.

Listing 5-25. Override CSS for GroupSummaryView

```
.x-grid3-row-alt{background-color:#FFFFCC;}

.x-grid3-body .x-grid3-td-car_value {
  background-color: #FFEEAA;
  border-right: 1px solid #FFFFFF;
}

.x-grid3-summary-row {
  background: #FFEEAA none repeat scroll 0% 50%;
  border-left: 1px solid #FFFFFF;
  color: #333333;
}

.x-grid3-summary-row .x-grid3-cell-inner {
  font-weight: bold;
  padding-bottom: 4px;
}
```

Note   An explanation of the CSS used in Listing 5-25 is beyond the scope of the book, but suffice to say that most web developers should be able to assist in the CSS tuning and tailoring needed to obtain the better effects shown in this example. The important point of this example is to show what can be done with a combination of the base GXT widgets and some additional CSS modifications.

The best way to play with and modify styles is to use the Firefox developer tool, called Firebug, which allows you to change style values and instantly see the results. This can show you what does and doesn't work when changing styles. It also shows you which internal GXT styles are being applied to a particular part of a widget.

Binders: Table, Tree, and TreeTable

As mentioned previously, there are a few widgets that do not support stores or ModelData directly. These widgets require you to either manually construct their child components yourself or utilize the Binder objects to bind a store and provide model support for child widgets automatically.

The com.extjs.gxt.ui.client.binder package contains five binders, each tailored to bind a store to a particular data widget. These binders follow:

- DataListBinder
- DataViewBinder
- TableBinder
- TreeBinder
- TreeTableBinder

Figure 5-7 provides an introduction to binders by illustrating an example of using the Tree widget with TreeBinder.

Figure 5-7. Tree using TreeBinder

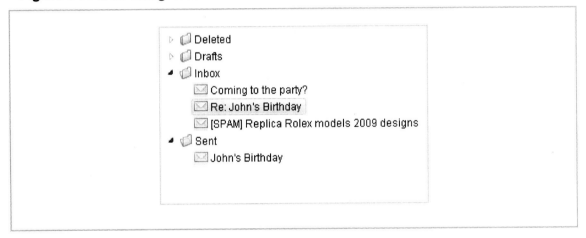

Tree is a hierarchical data widget, and therefore this will require a hierarchical implementation of store, such as TreeStore. Additionally, you need to have a ModelData implementation that understands the concept of parent and child nodes, such as BaseTreeModel.

Constructing the relationship is fairly logical, and Listing 5-26 outlines what you'll use in Listing 5-27.

Listing 5-26. BaseTreeModel

```
BaseTreeModel btmParent = new BaseTreeModel();
btmParent.set("name", "Parent's Display Name");

BaseTreeModel btm = new BaseTreeModel();
btm.set("name", "1st Child's Display Name ");
btmParent.add(btm);
```

```
btm = new BaseTreeModel();
btm.set("name", "2nd Child's Display Name ");
btmParent.add(btm);

...

modelArrayList.add(btmParent);
```

When you've created all your parents and added the child models to them, you can then add all the parents to TreeStore.

Listing 5-27. TreeStore

```
TreeStore<BaseTreeModel> store;
store = new TreeStore<BaseTreeModel>();
store.add(CodeSnippet.getTreeModels(), true);
```

You then create an instance of a Tree widget, and define some of its style information. In this case, you set an icon to display against the leaf child nodes (models that have no children themselves).

Listing 5-28. Tree

```
Tree tree = new Tree();
tree.getStyle().setLeafIconStyle("icon-email");
```

The final step is to create a TreeBinder and bind the Tree and store. You tell the binder to automatically load all children as needed and set the display property so that the TreeItems have the correct display label.

The last line initializes the binder and builds the tree.

Listing 5-29. TreeStore

```
TreeBinder binder = new TreeBinder(tree, store);
binder.setAutoLoad(true);
binder.setDisplayProperty("name");
binder.init();
```

So, apart from adding the Tree to a container and attaching it to RootPanel, there is no further configuration needed.

Of course, this only provides an introduction to Tree, and there are many other useful things you can do (such as combining it with Drag-n-Drop, menus, and events).

Summary

At roughly a fifth of the book's content, we covered a lot of complex examples: stores, models, and loaders, combined with an introduction to GWT's RPC mechanism. We then jumped into Grid and covered editing, grouping, and summary support. We finally ended with an introduction to Binder and a Tree example.

I have no doubt that, by now, you're ready to see all this new GXT information assembled into a full working example. In the next chapter, we'll combine most of what you've seen here, plus a few new tricks, into a customer contacts database.

Chapter 6: A Working Example

In this final chapter we'll step through a complete, functional application. Modeled on a typical customer contact database application, it is titled "myCustomerContacts," as shown in Figure 6-1. This application allows users to search for existing users (by name, address, or e-mail), add or delete users, and update existing customer records.

The application will mainly use widgets you've seen in previous chapters, plus a few new widgets that are easier to explain in a full working example. You'll also get a better understanding of how to use widgets together, binding common functionality to achieve a rich Internet application experience with a minimum of coding effort.

Figure 6-1. The myCustomerContacts application

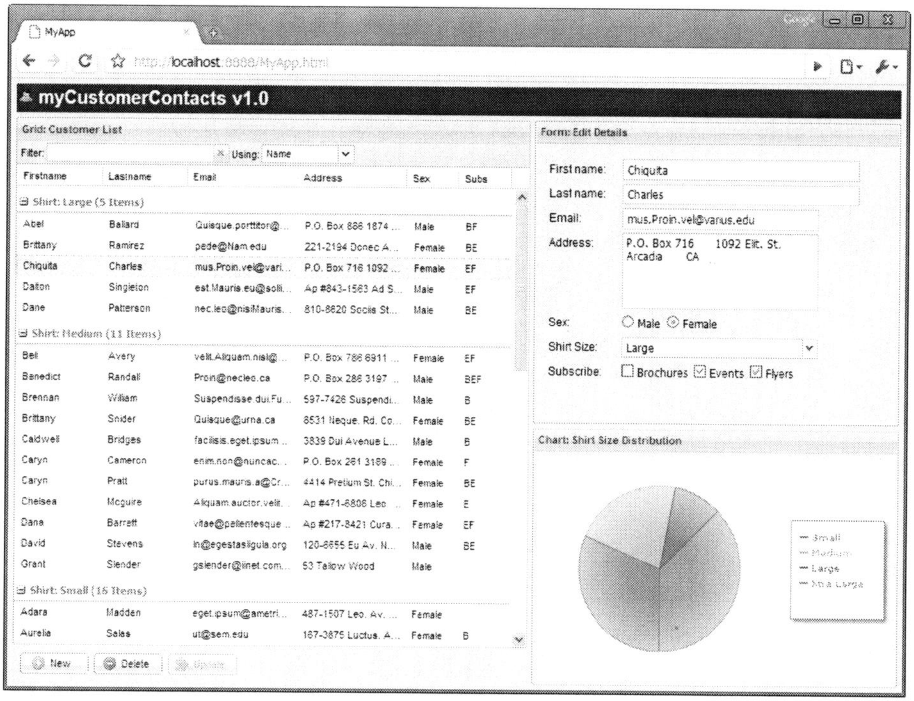

myCustomerContacts Application—What's New?

The application contains many widgets and components that have been covered in the previous chapters, but also some new things that haven't been covered so far. These are as follows:

- **FormBinding**: The ability to bind forms and fields to stores.
- **Charts**: A new feature in GXT 2.0 that adds a full interactive charting widget.
- **Store updates**: Data that is modified is committed back to the server.

The code discussed in this chapter was added to the base MyApp project created in Chapter 2, keeping as much of that application's setup and configuration as possible. As such, only the most significant and relevant changes will be covered, though you can still get the application running as the full and working source is provided with the book.

You can see a full and working version of this application by visiting
`http://extjs.com/myCustomerContacts`.

When Loading

When GWT applications get larger, there is sometimes a delay while the application code and resources are loaded and executed. To provide the user with a response during this delay, you can add a loading HTML fragment, as shown in Figure 6-2.

Figure 6-2. Loading fragment

This HTML is within the static page and will be rendered by the browser almost immediately, before any JavaScript is loaded or executed. The HTML fragment is placed within the <body> elements of the page.

Listing 6-1 provides the code to build the HTML fragment.

Listing 6-1. Loading HTML Fragment

```
<style>
#loading {
position: absolute; left: 45%; top: 40%; padding: 2px;
margin-left:-45px; z-index:20001; border:1px solid #ccc;
}
#loading .loading-indicator {
background:#eef;font:bold 13px tahoma,arial,helvetica;
padding:10px;margin:0;height:auto;color:#444;
}
#loading .loading-indicator img {
margin-right:8px; float:left; vertical-align:top;
}
#loading-msg {font:normal 10px arial,tahoma,sans-serif;}
</style>
<div id="loading">
<div class="loading-indicator">
<img src="gxt/images/default/shared/large-loading.gif"/>
myCustomerContacts<br />
<span id="loading-msg">Loading application...</span>
</div>
</div>
```

Note   The CSS associated with this loading HTML fragment also needs to be embedded in the same HTML page, otherwise it will not render completely until the required CSS resource has loaded. While this is not a best practice for web applications, to ensure you get your loading page to show as soon as possible, you need to make sure all resources are available as easily and quickly as possible.

Customer Data

Any application needs to work with data, and typically you should define this in advance. We'll continue to build on the Customer data model created in Chapter 5, and add a few more data types.

The class fields in Listing 6-2 have typical setters/getters, along with an appropriate class constructor to simplify Customer object creation.

Listing 6-2. Customer Fields

```java
private String email;
private String address;
private boolean male;
private SizeTypes shirt;
private int subscriptions;
```

The shirt field is a SizeTypes data type, which is an enumerated type that provides a flexible way to deal with shirt sizes. To facilitate simpler use with GXT, a toString method that returns the display text of the size was added. This type is defined in Listing 6-3.

Listing 6-3. SizeTypes Enumerated Type

```java
public enum SizeTypes {

    SMALL("Small"), MEDIUM("Medium"),
    LARGE("Large"), XTRA_LARGE("Xtra Large");

    private String size;

    SizeTypes(String size) {
        this.size = size;
    }

    public String toString() {
        return size;
    }
}
```

The subscriptions field, a simple integer value, also has an enumerated type that assists with the conversion and handling of subscriptions. MarketingTypes is defined in Listing 6-4.

Listing 6-4. MarketingTypes Enumerated Type

```java
public enum MarketingTypes {

    BROCHURES(0x1,"Brochures"), EVENTS(0x2,"Events"),
    ANNOUNCEMENTS(0x4,"Announcements");

    private int type;
    private String name;

    MarketingTypes(int type,String name) {
        this.type = type;
        this.name = name;
    }
```

```
public int intValue() {
  return type;
}

public String toString() {
  return name;
}
}
```

Keeping Data Independent

In Chapter 5 I discussed the benefit of using the GXT BeanModel and how it is possible to use domain objects without having to transfer data into (and out of) ModelData objects, letting GWT do the heavy lifting of generating new data types for use with GXT.

In this application, the Customer object and the related data types are all located in an independent package, allowing the server implementation to be completely independent of GXT. Technically, the server implementation does not need a reference to anything other than the GWT servlet code and the previously defined data types.

To enable this independent package scope within the GWT client application, add the following lines to the GWT XML module file:

```
<module rename-to='myapp'>
  ...
  <source path="data"/>
  <source path="client"/>
</module>
```

Classes associated with the data model can now be located in the package com.apress.data, keeping our data and client code independent.

Layout and Construction

Visually, the application has four panels: a title shown at the top, a list of customers on the left side, and a panel on the right side that contains two panels—the top half a form and the bottom half a chart.

Nested layouts are used to achieve this result, as shown in Figure 6-3, and are combined together to attain the layout and panel behavior desired for this kind of application.

Specifically, two BorderLayouts are arranged such that the first handles the outer northern, center, and eastern regions; and the second is within the eastern region, handling the inner northern and center regions.

The outer eastern region and the inner northern region are configured with split bars so that you can resize the regions, but a constraint on the minimum sizes keeps the "*3. Form*" panel at a size suitable for viewing its fields.

Figure 6-3. The layout

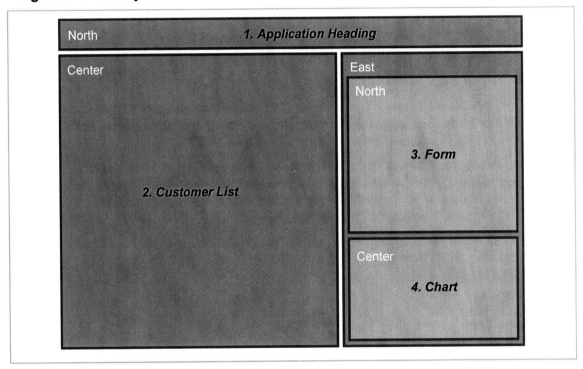

Internally, the application is constructed using sections of code focused on the following tasks:

- onModuleLoad: The initial entry point section defined by GWT.

- prepareServices: Configures services and prepares the local store.

- buildMainLayout: Configures/builds the application nested layouts.

- buildGridPanel: Configures and constructs the Grid panel.

- buildFormPanel: Configures and constructs the Form panel.

- buildChartPanel: Configures and constructs the Chart panel.

- showNewDialog: Creates and shows a dialog.

Only a small amount of CSS has been used to demonstrate that most of the visual configuration can be performed with the base GXT widgets and components.

The major addition to the CSS is the appHeading style, which places an image, and sets the background color, text color, text size, and margins and padding needed to show the application title correctly.

Also, three icons that are used by buttons within the application have been added. Adding icons via CSS was covered in Chapter 3.

Listing 6-5 outlines the code for these additions.

Listing 6-5. MyApp.css

```
* {
  font-family: arial, helvetica, tahoma, sans-serif;
}
.text {
  font-size: 12px;
}
.appHeading {
  background:#15428B url(images/user.png) no-repeat center left !important;
  color:#ffffff;
  font-size:20px;
  font-weight:bold;
  padding:2;
  margin-bottom:2;
  text-indent:15px
}
.icon-new {
  background: url(images/new.gif) no-repeat center left !important;
}
.icon-delete {
  background: url(images/delete.gif) no-repeat center left !important;
}
.icon-update {
  background: url(images/update.png) no-repeat center left !important;
}
```

When the Module Loads

The public method onModuleLoad is where all GWT (and GXT) applications begin, the main entry point to the application. This section is the core part of our application where we build, configure, and connect our application components together.

The first thing you need to do before any GXT widget is created is configure the theme you wish to use. In this case, the default theme for our application will be Blue. Ensure that the setting is forced, to override any previous theme preference saved in the StateManager.

Next, you call all of the other application sections: prepare the services, create a Viewport, construct and build the main layouts (the Grid, Form, and Chart panels), and then attach the Viewport to the GWT RootPanel.

Attaching the Viewport renders the application. This is always a good place to remove the HTML loading message using a static GXT method, which hides the tag with an ID of loading, including all children—effectively hiding the entire loading HTML fragment.

Finally, you ask the store's loader to load the data from the remote server. This is performed last to ensure the application has had a chance to render before you start requesting data. Listing 6-6 shows the complete onModuleLoad code.

Listing 6-6. onModuleLoad Listing

```
public void onModuleLoad() {
  GXT.setDefaultTheme(Theme.BLUE, true);

  prepareServices();
  Viewport viewport = new Viewport();
  buildMainLayout(viewport);
  buildGridPanel();
  buildFormPanel();
  buildChartPanel();
  RootPanel.get().add(viewport);
  GXT.hideLoadingPanel("loading");

  loader.load();
}
```

Preparing for Services

In this section of code, you establish the client side of the RPC service definitions. The services are described later in this chapter, but essentially the server implementation is similar to what we covered in Chapter 5.

The code in Listing 6-7 sets up the service definition and sets the service entry point, which matches the configured service within the Servlet web.xml configuration file. The code in Listing 6-8 is a fairly typical GWT RPC client configuration for a service.

Listing 6-7. Setup Services

```
service = (MyServiceAsync) GWT.create(MyService.class);
ServiceDefTarget endpoint = (ServiceDefTarget) service;
String moduleRelativeURL = GWT.getModuleBaseURL();
moduleRelativeURL += "myService";
endpoint.setServiceEntryPoint(moduleRelativeURL);
```

Next, you configure RpcProxy, Reader, and ListLoader to use BeanModel types. RpcProxy is set up to call getCustomers(), which is defined in the service interfaces. Listing 6-8 is similar to what you saw in Chapter 5.

Listing 6-8. Configure Proxy, Reader, and Loader

```
RpcProxy<BeanModel> proxy = new RpcProxy<BeanModel>() {
  @Override
  public void load(Object loadConfig,
    AsyncCallback callback) {
    service.getCustomers(callback);
  }
};
BeanModelReader reader = new BeanModelReader();
loader = new BaseListLoader(proxy, reader);
```

When you configure the store, use GroupingStore so that you can group on "shirt." You should also add a StoreListener so that you can update a status bar and/or Chart panel based on the changed contents of the store.

Listing 6-9 demonstrates how to configure the store.

Listing 6-9. Configure Store

```
store = new GroupingStore<BeanModel>(loader);
store.groupBy("shirt");
store.addStoreListener(new StoreListener<BeanModel>() {

public void storeRemove(StoreEvent<BeanModel> se) {
  updateStatus();
  updateChartTask.delay(DEFAULT_DELAY);
}

public void storeUpdate(StoreEvent<BeanModel> se) {
  if (se.getRecord().isModified("shirt")) {
    updatingStore = true;
    store.groupBy("shirt", true);
    grid.getView().refresh(false);
    updatingStore = false;
  }
  updateStatus();
  updateChartTask.delay(DEFAULT_DELAY);
}

public void storeDataChanged(StoreEvent<BeanModel> se) {
  if (!updatingStore) {
    updateStatus();
```

```
    updateChartTask.delay(DEFAULT_DELAY);
  }
}

public void storeFilter(StoreEvent<BeanModel> se) {
  updateChartTask.delay(DEFAULT_DELAY);
}
});

updateChartTask = new DelayedTask(new Listener() {
  public void handleEvent(BaseEvent be) {
    updateChart();
  }
});
```

The implementation of updateChart is provided later in this chapter. The updateStatus code essentially refreshes a status message and, like the updateChart method, is performed when the store data changes.

In the StoreListener code in Listing 6-9, you will see that within the storeUpdate method is a detection of the change to a particular property field within the model, in this case, "shirt." When this field is modified, you also have to regroup the store, and this in turn generates Store.DataChanged events. To avoid updating twice, an updating flag is used to ignore the additional event.

Also, a GXT DelayedTask is used to dampen repeated update events that would update the chart. DelayedTask is essentially a more useful implementation of GWT Timer: it cancels the existing timer if DelayedTask.delay(int) is called again. In the full listing, DEFAULT_DELAY is given a value of 500, which is half a second.

Note   Why did you have to regroup the store? When you modify the property value that GroupingView is using to group by, you need to regroup the store so that the modified row is sorted correctly within it. GroupingStore is really a special-purpose, sorted store, and this regroup ensures all related "grouped" fields are logically grouped together.

In Listing 6-10, the number of modified records is obtained from the store. If the number is more than zero, the status text is updated and the update button is enabled; otherwise, the status text is cleared and the button is disabled.

Listing 6-10. Update Status

```
private void updateStatus() {
    int numModRec = store.getModifiedRecords().size();
    if (numModRec > 0) {
        gridButBar.getUpdateButton().setEnabled(true);
        gridButBar.setStatusText(numModRec + " rows modified");
    } else {
        gridButBar.getUpdateButton().setEnabled(false);
        gridButBar.setStatusText("");
    }
}
```

The preparation of services is complete. In summary, you set up the service definitions; plug the Proxy, Reader, and Loader together; and create a GroupingStore with an appropriate listener defined to notify you when certain store events occur.

Building the Main Layout

The main layout is constructed in three steps: set up the main panels (or containers), configure the inner layout, and finally set up the outer layout.

Listing 6-11 shows the code associated with setting up the panels, which is fairly generic.

Listing 6-11. Set Up the Panels

```
LayoutContainer inner = new LayoutContainer();
LayoutContainer appHeading = new LayoutContainer();
appHeading.addText("myCustomerContacts v1.0");
appHeading.addStyleName("appHeading");
gridPanel = new ContentPanel();
gridPanel.setHeading("Grid: Customer List");
gridPanel.setBodyBorder(false);
formPanel = new FormPanel();
formPanel.setHeading("Form: Edit Details");
chartPanel = new ContentPanel();
chartPanel.setHeading("Chart: Shirt Size Distribution");
```

Using the style tag appHeading, defined in CSS, places all image, style, and color information outside of the code and allows a developer to update this information without having to recompile the application—an important aspect of any web development.

Listing 6-12 configures the layouts and sets the minimum and maximum sizes for the regions.

Listing 6-12. *Configure the Inner Layout*

```
BorderLayoutData inNorth = new BorderLayoutData(LayoutRegion.NORTH, 320);
inNorth.setMinSize(320);
inNorth.setMaxSize(600);
inNorth.setSplit(true);
BorderLayoutData inCenter = new BorderLayoutData(LayoutRegion.CENTER);
inCenter.setMargins(new Margins(5, 0, 0, 0));
inner.setLayout(new BorderLayout());
inner.add(formPanel, inNorth);
inner.add(chartPanel, inCenter);
```

Listing 6-13 configures the outer layout, again setting the minimum and maximum allowable sizing for the region. This is important because you need to keep a minimum amount of size to correctly display the form's fields. Allowing the region to become too small will result in some fields being removed from the form (and will obviously make the form unusable).

The last part of Listing 6-13 actually adds the panels to the Viewport and completes the high-level main layout of the application.

Listing 6-13. *Configure the Outer Layout*

```
BorderLayoutData north = new BorderLayoutData(LayoutRegion.NORTH, 30);
north.setMargins(new Margins(5, 5, 0, 5));
BorderLayoutData outCenter = new BorderLayoutData(LayoutRegion.CENTER);
outCenter.setMargins(new Margins(5));
BorderLayoutData east = new BorderLayoutData(LayoutRegion.EAST, 400);
east.setMinSize(400);
east.setMaxSize(600);
east.setSplit(true);
east.setMargins(new Margins(5, 5, 5, 0));
viewport.setLayout(new BorderLayout());
viewport.add(appHeading, north);
viewport.add(gridPanel, outCenter);
viewport.add(inner, east);
```

Building the Grid Panel

As shown in Figure 6-4, the Grid panel is conceptually constructed with three sets of widgets.

First is a ToolBar with a StoreFilterField and SimpleComboBox. These widgets provide filtering support to aid in searching or restricting the available models within the store. Second is the grid itself, configured with GroupingView. Third, a row of buttons is added to the panel.

Figure 6-4. The Grid panel

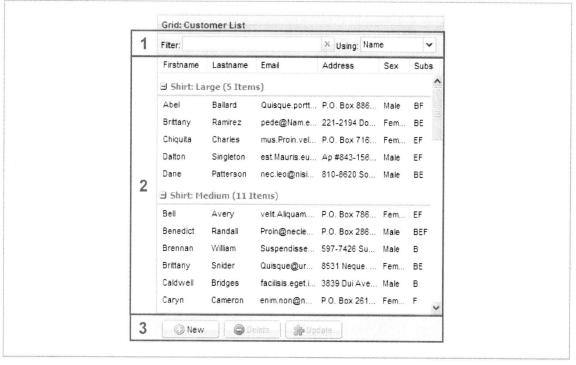

ToolBar is set as the panel's top component. The grid is just added to the panel set with a FitLayout, and the buttons are added as part of the panel's built-in button bar.

After the ToolBar is created, the filter, combo box, and appropriate labels are added together.

Listing 6-14 shows the code associated with creating the ToolBar.

Listing 6-14. Creating a ToolBar

```
// build the toolbar
ToolBar bar = new ToolBar();
bar.add(new LabelToolItem("Filter:"));
bar.add(field);
bar.add(new LabelToolItem("Using:"));
bar.add(filterUsing);
```

SimpleComboBox is not really anything new. The idea of this combo box is to allow the user to choose what aspect of the Customer data to filter on—Name, Email, or Address.

Listing 6-15 shows the code associated with creating the SimpleComboBox.

Listing 6-15. Creating a SimpleComboBox

```
final SimpleComboBox<String> filterUsing = new SimpleComboBox<String>();
filterUsing.setEditable(false);
filterUsing.setWidth(100);
filterUsing.add("Name");
filterUsing.add("Email");
filterUsing.add("Address");
filterUsing.setSimpleValue("Name");
```

The StoreFilterField is essentially a text field, which is bound to a store so that it can filter the store's contents based on the text entered.

StoreFilterField does the filtering based on the return value of its doSelect method. In Listing 6-16, depending on the selected value of the SimpleComboBox (filterUsing), the associated model values will be matched against the filter's String value—true is returned if a match is found.

Listing 6-16 shows the code associated with creating the StoreFilterField.

Listing 6-16. Creating a StoreFilterField

```
StoreFilterField<BeanModel> field = new StoreFilterField<BeanModel>() {
  protected boolean doSelect(Store<BeanModel> store,
BeanModel parent, BeanModel record, String property, String filter) {
    Customer cust = record.getBean();
    switch (filterUsing.getSelectedIndex()) {
    case 0:
    String firstname = cust.getFirstname().toLowerCase();
      if (firstname.startsWith(filter.toLowerCase())) {
        return true;
      }
    String lastname = cust.getLastname().toLowerCase();
      if (lastname.startsWith(filter.toLowerCase())) {
        return true;
      }
      break;
    case 1:
      String email = cust.getEmail().toLowerCase();
      if (email.indexOf(filter.toLowerCase()) != -1) {
        return true;
      }
      break;
    case 2:
      String addr = cust.getAddress().toLowerCase();
```

```
      if (addr.indexOf(filter.toLowerCase()) != -1) {
        return true;
      }
      break;
    }
    return false;
  }
};
field.setWidth(200);
field.bind(store);
```

Then the parts needed for a functioning grid with a GroupingView are built and created. We've covered grids fairly comprehensively previously, so Listing 6-17 only shows a section where a custom GridCellRenderer is used.

Listing 6-17. Constructing the Grid: Columns

```
column = new ColumnConfig();
column.setId("male");
column.setHeader("Sex");
column.setRenderer(new GridCellRenderer<BeanModel>() {
  public String render(BeanModel model, String property, ColumnData config, int rowIndex,
      int colIndex, ListStore<BeanModel> store) {
    boolean b = (Boolean) model.get(property);
    return b ? "Male" : "Female";
  }
});
column.setWidth(50);
columns.add(column);
```

In Listing 6-17, the model contains a Boolean value that you want to render as Male or Female instead of true or false. This is performed by obtaining the model value and, depending on the value, returning the text you wish to display in the column.

Listing 6-18 shows the construction of the GroupingView.

Listing 6-18. Constructing the Grid: GroupingView

```
GroupingView view = new GroupingView();
view.setGroupRenderer(new GridGroupRenderer() {
  public String render(GroupColumnData data) {
    int s = data.models.size();
    String f = cm.getColumnById(data.field).getHeader();
    String l = s == 1 ? "Item" : "Items";
    return f + ": " +data.group+ " (" +s+ " " +l+ ")";
  }
});
view.setForceFit(true);
view.setShowGroupedColumn(false);
```

The GridGroupRenderer is similar to the GridCellRenderer used previously. The returned value produces text like *Shirt: Large (6 items)*.

The view is also told to force column widths to fit all the available space and hide the column that is grouped.

OK, we're up to the creation of the grid itself.

The view is set, and the selection mode is set to SINGLE. Now you add a selection listener that assigns a global field selectedModel. That way, you always know which model is currently selected (which is important for when the user selects the delete button).

If the selected model is not null (something has been selected), bind the form to the current model. If the selected model is null (nothing is selected), unbind the form and disable it. The delete button's enabled state is also toggled based on the selected model value.

Note   FormBinding, what it is and how it works, is explained later in the "Building the Form Panel" section.

Listing 6-19 shows the construction of the grid.

Listing 6-19. Constructing the Grid: The Grid

```
grid = new Grid<BeanModel>(store, cm);
grid.setView(view);
grid.getSelectionModel().setSelectionMode(SelectionMode.SINGLE);
grid.getSelectionModel().addListener(Events.SelectionChange,
  new Listener<SelectionChangedEvent<BeanModel>>() {
    public void handleEvent (SelectionChangedEvent<BeanModel> be) {
```

```
    selectedModel = be.getSelectedItem();
    if (selectedModel != null) {
      formBindings.bind(selectedModel);
      formPanel.setEnabled(true);
      gridButBar.getDeleteButton().setEnabled(true);
    } else {
      formPanel.setEnabled(false);
      formBindings.unbind();
      gridButBar.getDeleteButton().setEnabled(false);
    }
  }
});
```

Listing 6-20 shows that building the panel is simply a matter of setting the layout then adding the toolbar and grid. The update and delete buttons are initially disabled. Certain events within the application will enable these buttons for use when appropriate.

Listing 6-20. Building the Grid Panel

```
gridPanel.setLayout(new FitLayout());
gridPanel.setTopComponent(bar);
gridPanel.add(grid);
gridPanel.setButtonAlign(HorizontalAlignment.LEFT);
gridButBar = new GridButBar(gridPanel);
gridButBar.getUpdateButton().setEnabled(false);
gridButBar.getDeleteButton().setEnabled(false);
```

To simplify access to the three buttons added to the panel, a GridButBar class is used to basically create the buttons and hold the implementation of the selection events. Listing 6-21 outlines the GridButBar utility class.

Listing 6-21. GridButBar

```
public GridButBar(ContentPanel cp) {
  updBut.setIconStyle("icon-update");
  newBut.setIconStyle("icon-new");
  delBut.setIconStyle("icon-delete");
  cp.addButton(newBut);
  cp.addButton(delBut);
  cp.addButton(updBut);
  cp.addButton(new ButtonAdapter(statusMsg));

  updBut.addSelectionListener(...
  ...);

  newBut.addSelectionListener(...
  ...);
```

```
  delBut.addSelectionListener(...
  ...);
}

public Button getUpdateButton() {
  return updBut;
}

public Button getNewButton() {
  return newBut;
}

public Button getDeleteButton() {
  return delBut;
}

public void setStatusText(String text) {
  statusMsg.setHtml(text);
}
```

The missing addSelectionListener code for the buttons in Listing 6-21 is discussed later in the "Additional Bits" section, which covers what happens when an existing customer is deleted or updated, and when a new customer is created.

Building the Form Panel

FormBinding is a feature of GXT that hasn't been covered previously, so it's suitable to provide further explanation.

Using FormBinding (and FieldBinding), you can bind the change events of fields directly to a store and get live updating between the form and anything else, such as a grid, also using the store.

If all of your fields are simply text or number fields within a FormPanel and don't require validation, then you can use the auto-bind feature of FormBinding. Unfortunately, our application doesn't meet either requirement, so the application fields need to be manually added.

For a simple model and plain text field with no validation, use the code that follows:

```
TextField ln = new TextField();
ln.setName("lastname");
ln.setFieldLabel("Last name");
formBindings.addFieldBinding(new FieldBinding(ln, "lastname"));
```

As shown in Figure 6-5, the application uses field validation (such as the First name field not allowing blank values, and the Email field only allowing correctly formatted e-mail addresses).

Figure 6-5. The Form panel

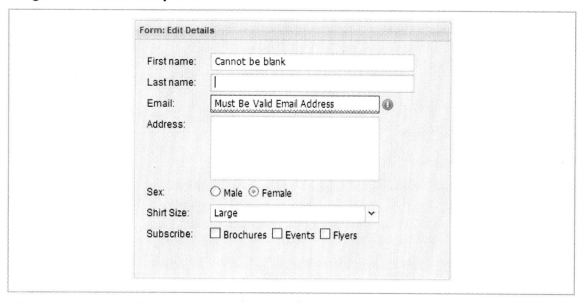

In the case of fields like the Male and Female radio buttons, you need to map the correct behavior back to the model based on the field values. So for the Male radio button, the value of true is already correct. For the Female radio button, you need to flip the Boolean value by setting the FieldBinding with a convertor, as shown in Listing 6-22.

Listing 6-22. Setting the FieldBinding with a Convertor

```
final Radio femaleRadio = new Radio();
femaleRadio.setName("radio");
femaleRadio.setBoxLabel("Female");
formBindings.addFieldBinding(new FieldBinding(femaleRadio, "male"));
formBindings.getBinding(femaleRadio).setConvertor(new Converter() {
  public Object convertModelValue(Object value) {
    return !((Boolean) value);
  }

  public Object convertFieldValue(Object value) {
    return !((Boolean) value);
  }
});
```

This will swap the changed Boolean state–obtained field and correctly set the model with the right value for this field.

For the SimpleComboBox that uses the SizeTypes data type, there is a GXT-supplied SimpleComboBoxFieldBinding that already knows how to deal with SimpleComboBox fields.

For the CheckBox fields, things get a little more complex. You need to convert from a Boolean checked value into a bitwise integer. To achieve FieldBinding support, you need to pass in some information about what each CheckBox field represents (in this case, it is that bitwise data) as follows:

```
check1.setData("bitvalue", 1);
...
check2.setData("bitvalue", 2);
...
check3.setData("bitvalue", 4);
```

Then you add a custom FieldBinding for each CheckBox field, as follows:

```
formBindings.addFieldBinding(new CustFldBnd(check1, "subs"));
formBindings.addFieldBinding(new CustFldBnd(check2, "subs"));
formBindings.addFieldBinding(new CustFldBnd(check3, "subs"));
```

The last part of the puzzle is the implementation of CustFldBnd. Listing 6-23 shows the custom FieldBinding code that correctly builds model or field values based on which CheckBox was selected and the model's original value.

Listing 6-23. Custom FieldBinding: CustFldBnd

```
public class CustFldBnd extends FieldBinding {
 public CustFldBnd(Field field, String property) {
  super(field, property);
 }

 public Object onConvertModelValue(Object value) {
  int bitvalue = (Integer) field.getData("bitvalue");
  return ((Integer) value & bitvalue) == bitvalue;
 }

 public Object onConvertFieldValue(Object value) {
  int bitvalue = (Integer) field.getData("bitvalue");
  int sub = (Integer) model.get(property) & ~bitvalue;
  sub |= ((Boolean) value ? bitvalue : 0);
  return new Integer(sub);
 }
}
```

The CustFldBnd class performs a similar function to the convertor used in the radio button field, but in this case, you are able to gain access to the underlying Field object when converting between the model value and the field value (and vice versa). As the Field object is accessible, the bitvalue can be obtained from the Field's getData method. The bitvalue is used to determine if that particular CheckBox field should be enabled or, if it was, what the resulting integer value should be.

Building the Chart Panel

Charts are a very new feature added in GXT 2.0. Unfortunately, there is not enough space to cover every possible chart type and feature, but you should be able to set up and configure most charts after this brief introduction and the example shown in the application.

The Chart widget is built on the OpenFlashChart library made available to the open source community. More information on this Flash library can be found at http://teethgrinder.co.uk/open-flash-chart-2/.

The GXT team has taken this Flash object and provided a comprehensive, interactive charting solution that can fully integrate with the GXT event system and the Store and ModelData data framework, and can be used like any other GXT widget.

Adding support for charts requires that you add the module inheritance in Listing 6-24 to your project.

Listing 6-24. MyApp.gwt.xml

```
<module rename-to='myapp'>
  ...
  <inherits name='com.extjs.gxt.charts.Chart' />
  ...
</module>
```

As shown in Figure 6-6, the application in this book is using a simple pie chart and graphically illustrates the distribution of shirt sizes across all customers. When data is updated within the store (either through FormBinding or new/deleted rows), the chart is updated instantly.

Figure 6-6. The Chart panel

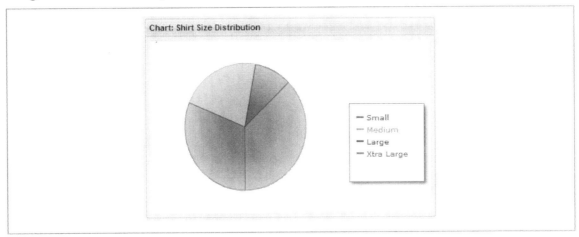

All charts can either be given JSON configuration data (based on the OFC API) or can use a GXT ChartModel that will process and build a JSON data string suitable for the OFC chart. The GXT ChartModel assists with building correctly formatted JSON data and saves you from having to remember the OFC API—you can simply set values as needed and achieve excellent-looking results with limited knowledge of the OFC API.

The Chart panel is not a complex configuration and simply uses FitLayout to position a Chart widget completely within the panel's available space.

Listing 6-25 shows how the panel is configured.

Listing 6-25. Building the Chart Panel

```
chartPanel.setLayout(new FitLayout());
chartPanel.setFrame(true);
chart = new Chart();
chartPanel.add(chart);
updateChart();
```

The real configuration details of the chart are within the updateChart() method, which is called when data is updated within the store.

In Listing 6-26, you'll see that when the chart is updated, the numShirts array that contains an accumulated count of each instance of SizeTypes within all the models is built. To achieve this, a list of models is obtained from the store and individually iterated over. This is one of the reasons why the updateChart method is called within a DelayedTask—not doing so will result in this code section being executed repeatedly, potentially producing a negative impact on browser performance.

The next part of Listing 6-26 builds a ChartModel and sets various options, such as background color and legend configuration. A PieChart object is created and configured, and then pie slices are added for every instance of SizeTypes. The value of each Slice is set via the numShirts array obtained previously. The label is obtained from the toString value of the SizeTypes data type.

Lastly, the ChartModel is given a chart configuration (the PieChart object), and the Chart widget is updated with the newly created ChartModel.

Listing 6-26. *updateChart*

```
int[] numShirts = new int[SizeTypes.values().length];
List<BeanModel> models = store.getModels();
for (BeanModel bm : models) {
  SizeTypes st = bm.get("shirt");
  numShirts[st.ordinal()]++;
}

ChartModel cm = new ChartModel();
cm.setBackgroundColour("#FCFCFC");
Legend lgd = new Legend(Position.RIGHT, true);
lgd.setMargin(10);
lgd.setPadding(10);
cm.setLegend(lgd);
PieChart pie = new PieChart();
pie.setAlpha(0.5f);
pie.setNoLabels(true);
pie.setTooltip("#label# #percent#<br>#val#");
pie.setAnimate(false);
pie.setAlphaHighlight(true);
pie.setGradientFill(true);
pie.setColours("#ff0000","#00aa00","#0000ff","#ff00ff");

int n = 0;
for (SizeTypes st : SizeTypes.values()) {
  String lbl = st.toString();
  pie.addSlices(new Slice(numShirts[n++], lbl, lbl));
}
cm.addChartConfig(pie);
if (chart != null) chart.setChartModel(cm);
```

Many other chart types, such as BarChart, AreaChart, LineChart, and RadarChart, are available. You can see a full list of charts within the GXT Explorer application (http://extjs.com/explorer).

GXT also provides sophisticated store support that allows you to simply identify the properties that should be bound to axis labels and values. Using the Chart widget's support for the store simplifies the notification and update of chart data when the store's data has changed internally.

Unfortunately, Chart does not currently support grouped data, as required by our application, so a custom update mechanism had to be implemented. Even so, the results are the same: when you tie a Chart to a StoreListener (as you've done), you can achieve some truly amazing interactive data visualization.

I guess this kind of interaction is expected of any comprehensive rich Internet application—lucky for us it was easy to do.

Additional Bits

There are a few additional items within the application that have not been explained. Most significant is the New Customer dialog, which shows when the user selects the New button.

The New Customer dialog, shown in Figure 6-7, is a combination of a Dialog with a FormPanel. A very polished and styled look is produced when you use this combination of widgets. For example, an inset is rendered around the field widgets that direct the user to the items that need to be completed before the dialog can be successfully saved and closed.

Figure 6-7. The New Customer dialog

Like most application dialogs, Dialog is modal and is given an icon to connect the window with the action just performed. Dialog is configured to be closable (meaning a close box shows at the top right of the heading), and the default CloseAction is defined to close, rather than just hide the widget.

Tip   The default behavior for Dialog is to hide on close, which does not destroy the window or any associated Dialog widget objects. Changing the default CloseAction to CLOSE instead of HIDE requires that the entire Dialog be created and re-opened again, which may take longer to execute and render each time.

Either option is acceptable, but depending on the frequency of use, you may wish to consider leaving the default CloseAction set to HIDE. This means, though, that you'll need to manage the reset or clearing of previously used internal widgets when you reuse a hidden Dialog.

New Customers

As the FormPanel is enclosed within a Dialog, there is no need to include a header on the panel, and so in Listing 6-27, the panel is configured with borders, body borders, and header visibility all set to false.

Listing 6-27 produces the New Customer dialog.

Listing 6-27. New Customers: Dialog

```
final Dialog newDialog = new Dialog();
newDialog.setModal(true);
newDialog.setPlain(true);
newDialog.setIconStyle("icon-new");
newDialog.setHeading("New Customer");
newDialog.setSize(450, 170);
newDialog.setClosable(true);
newDialog.setCloseAction(CloseAction.CLOSE);
newDialog.setLayout(new FitLayout());

FormPanel panel = new FormPanel();
panel.setBorders(false);
panel.setBodyBorder(false);
panel.setPadding(5);
panel.setHeaderVisible(false);

Button save = new Button("Save");
save.addSelectionListener(new SelectionListener<ButtonEvent>() {
  public void componentSelected(ButtonEvent ce) {
    Field fn = (Field) newDialog.getItems().get(0);
    Field ln = (Field) newDialog.getItems().get(1);
    Field em = (Field) newDialog.getItems().get(2);
```

```
    if (fn.isValid() && em.isValid()) {
      ...
    }
  }
});
```

When the user selects the New Customer dialog's Save button, the dialog's field values are retrieved and checked for validation. If the firstname (fn) and email (em) fields are valid, the customer data is saved using the code in Listing 6-28.

Listing 6-28. New Customers: Service

```
Customer c = new Customer();
c.setFirstname((String) fn.getValue());
c.setLastname((String) ln.getValue());
c.setEmail((String) em.getValue());
BeanModelFactory factory = BeanModelLookup.get().getFactory(Customer.class);
selectedModel = factory.createModel(c);

Map<String, Customer> save = new HashMap<String, Customer>();
save.put(c.getEmail(),c);

AsyncCallback<Boolean> aCallback = new  AsyncCallback<Boolean>() {
  public void onFailure(Throwable caught) {
  }

  public void onSuccess(Boolean result) {
    if (result) {
      store.add(selectedModel);
      formBindings.bind(selectedModel);
      grid.getSelectionModel().select(selectedModel);
      newDialog.close();
    }
  }
};
service.updateSaveCustomers(save, aCallback);
```

To save a customer, a new Customer object is created and the values filled. Next, a BeanModel factory is used to create a new instance of a Customer BeanModel object. This object is eventually used to add the newly created customer to the store, so it appears in the Grid and Chart panels.

The Customer object is placed into a HashMap, which is used by the server's updateSaveCustomers service to update (or insert) customer data. A callback is created that, upon success, adds the BeanModel to the store, binds the form, and selects the model within the grid.

Update Customers

When models within the store are modified, the Update Customer button is enabled. When the button is selected, a MessageBox is created, asking the user whether to commit all modified records (Yes), reject the commit (No), or cancel the commit (Cancel). Listing 6-29 shows the creation of the MessageBox.

Listing 6-29. Update Customers: Yes, No, or Cancel

```
String msg = "Yes to commit all changes, "
  + "No to reject all changes, or Cancel";
MessageBox box = new MessageBox();
box.setTitle("Update modified rows?");
box.setMessage(msg);
box.addListener(Events.Close, callback);
box.setIcon(MessageBox.QUESTION);
box.setButtons(MessageBox.YESNOCANCEL);
box.show();
```

The callback defined in the MessageBox confirms which button was selected. If the selection is Yes, the code in Listing 6-30 is executed. If the selection is No, store.rejectChanges() is called, rejecting and resetting all change records to their prior state. If the selection is Cancel, nothing occurs and the MessageBox closes.

Listing 6-30. Update Customers: Service

```
AsyncCallback<Boolean> aCallback = new AsyncCallback<Boolean>() {
  public void onFailure(Throwable caught) {
  }

  public void onSuccess(Boolean result) {
    if (result) {
      store.commitChanges();
    }
  }
};
service.updateSaveCustomers(getStoreChanges(), aCallback);
```

The server's updateSaveCustomers service is again used to update the store's changed models. These models are obtained using the code in Listing 6-31.

Listing 6-31. Getting the Store Changes

```
private Map<String, Customer> getStoreChanges() {
  Map<String, Customer> changes;
  changes = new HashMap<String, Customer>();
  for (Record r : store.getModifiedRecords()) {
```

```
      BeanModel bm = (BeanModel) r.getModel();
      String email = bm.get("email");
      if (r.isModified("email")) {
        email = (String) r.getChanges().get("email");
      }
      changes.put(email, (Customer) bm.getBean());
    }
    return changes;
  }
```

The code in Listing 6-31 simply builds a HashMap of all modified records, ensuring each Customer stored in the HashMap is keyed with the original e-mail address. `Record.getChanges()` provides a list of the original values.

Delete Customers

When the user selects the Delete Customer button, the `removeCustomer` service is used to delete the customer record from the server's persistent store.

The Customer record to be removed is identified by the last selected model set by the grid `SelectionModel` listener. Listing 6-32 shows the code for the service call.

Listing 6-32. Delete Customers: Service

```
AsyncCallback<Boolean> aCallback = new AsyncCallback<Boolean>() {
  public void onFailure(Throwable caught) {
  }

  public void onSuccess(Boolean result) {
    if (result) {
      store.remove(selectedModel);
      grid.getSelectionModel().deselectAll();
    }
  }
};
service.removeCustomer((Customer)selectedModel.getBean(),aCallback);
```

Listing 6-33 shows the code for the Are You Sure? MessageBox.

Listing 6-33. Delete Customers: Are you sure?

```
String msg = "Are you sure you wish to permanently "
  + "delete this customer record?";
MessageBox.confirm("Delete Customer?", msg, callback);
```

The Server Code

All that remains is a brief overview of the server side of the application's RemoteServlet code. In a real application, you'll no doubt have a comprehensive data management and persistence layer configured. In this simple application, data is written to a simple comma-separated value (CSV) file that loads and saves the entire list as needed.

Listing 6-34 shows the code that gets, removes, and updates customers.

Listing 6-34. Get, Remove, and Update Customers

```java
public List<Customer> getCustomers() {
  if (customers == null) {
    loadCustomers();
  }
  return new ArrayList<Customer>(customers.values());
}

public Boolean removeCustomer(Customer c) {
  if (customers.remove(c.getEmail()) != null) {
    return saveCustomers();
  }
  return false;
}

public Boolean updateSaveCustomers(Map<String, Customer> changes) {
  for (String origEmail : changes.keySet()) {
    customers.remove(origEmail);
    Customer newUpdated = changes.get(origEmail);
    customers.put(newUpdated.getEmail(), newUpdated);
  }
  return saveCustomers();
}
```

Summary

You've now got a functional application that covers most of the user aspects typically expected of a rich Internet application. I introduced the FormBinding and Chart widgets and combined these new items with things covered in previous chapters.

We've reached the end of the book, and unfortunately we still haven't covered every single part of the GXT library. We covered the Google Web Toolkit, a bunch of widgets ranging from Buttons to Grids, and how to build a complete and functional rich Internet application.

GXT has many other aspects that just couldn't be explored within the pages of this book. Some of these features follow:

- **MVC**: A model-view-controller framework that, for advanced/larger applications, provides a messaging system to keep your data model, controller logic, and view widgets all logically independent.

- **Desktop**: A framework for simulating a full desktop experience, built within the browser. Typically used in cases where a full web-desktop experience is needed (i.e., multiple subapplications where users can launch applications like they would in a full desktop operating system). As a web application, this provides the user with a similar experience to their existing desktop, but delivered via the Web.

- **Charts**: In this book we only dipped slightly into the full comprehensive charting library included in GXT 2.0. There are a range of bar charts (3D, Glass, Horizontal, Cylindrical); line, area, and scatter point charts; and full support for configuring the X,Y axis, including a Radar-style spider-radial axis.

- **Tree/Table**: While we looked at a Tree example, there is a fair amount more you can do with Tree. Also, a TreeTable widget combines the best features of the Tree and Table widgets into a composite data widget.

So while I covered a significant amount of the GXT library within this book, there is still much more to be discovered. I strongly recommend that you visit the GXT Explorer and Samples sections of the Ext JS web site for more information and examples.

So go visit `http://extjs.com/products/gxt/`, and keep building.

Copyright

Developing with Ext GWT: Enterprise RIA Development

© 2009 by Grant Slender

ISBN-13 (electronic): 978-1-4302-1941-5

ISBN-13 (paperback): 978-1-4302-1940-8

Trademarked names may appear in this book. Rather than use a trademark symbol with every occurrence of a trademarked name, we use the names only in an editorial fashion and to the benefit of the trademark owner, with no intention of infringement of the trademark.

Distributed to the book trade in the United States by Springer-Verlag New York, Inc., 233 Spring Street, 6th Floor, New York, NY 10013, and outside the United States by Springer-Verlag GmbH & Co. KG, Tiergartenstr. 17, 69112 Heidelberg, Germany.

In the United States: phone 1-800-SPRINGER, fax 201-348-4505, e-mail orders@springer-ny.com, or visit http://www.springer-ny.com. Outside the United States: fax +49 6221 345229, e-mail orders@springer.de, or visit http://www.springer.de.

For information on translations, please contact Apress directly at 2855 Telegraph Ave, Suite 600, Berkeley, CA 94705. Phone 510-549-5930, fax 510-549-5939, e-mail info@apress.com, or visit http://www.apress.com.

CPSIA information can be obtained at www.ICGtesting.com

226009LV00009B/19/P